MW00903802

I Love to Tell the Story

A Memoir

Susan Barnett Braun

Copyright © 2011 Susan Barnett Braun
All rights reserved.
ISBN: 1467931187
ISBN-13: 978-1467931182

To Caroline, Isabel, and Sophie …
who love to listen

TABLE OF CONTENTS

I Love To Tell the Story

I love to tell the story of unseen things above,
of Jesus and his glory, of Jesus and his love.
I love to tell the story, because I know 'tis true;
it satisfies my longings as nothing else can do.

I love to tell the story; 'tis pleasant to repeat
what seems, each time I tell it, more wonderfully sweet.
I love to tell the story, for some have never heard
the message of salvation from God's own holy Word.

I love to tell the story, for those who know it best
seem hungering and thirsting to hear it like the rest.
And when, in scenes of glory, I sing the new, new song,
'twill be the old, old story that I have loved so long.

I love to tell the story, 'twill be my theme in glory,
to tell the old, old story of Jesus and his love.

Chapter 1 – Come Ye Sinners, Poor and Needy

There is always one moment in childhood when the door opens and lets the future in.

-Graham Greene

Come, ye sinners, poor and needy, weak and wounded, sick and sore;
Jesus ready stands to save you, full of pity, love, and pow'r.
I will arise and go to Jesus, He will embrace me in His arms;
In the arms of my dear Savior, O, there are ten thousand charms.

This was it. The big day. I shifted back and forth, scratching an itch that had just popped up. *Now!* All I had to do was walk to the front of the First Baptist Church sanctuary and tell Dr. Silver that I wanted Jesus to be my Savior. Simple as that.

Come, ye thirsty, come, and welcome, God's free bounty glorify;
True belief and true repentance, every grace that brings you nigh.

I will arise and go to Jesus, He will embrace me in His arms;
In the arms of my dear Savior, O, there are ten thousand charms.

The organ and piano's melancholy, minor notes heightened my anxiety. I dug my fingernails into the pew ahead of me, where they made little dents in the wax. *Go! Just go!* I wanted to be a Christian. I had imagined this moment many times, but somehow, walking down that aisle now seemed impossible. Going to the front of the church! In front of all those people! I glanced up at the spinning ceiling fans, cooling the sanctuary as they spun and spun and spun. Little beads of sweat rolled down the back of my neck, and it felt awfully warm for the first week of June.

Let not conscience make you linger, nor of fitness fondly dream;
All the fitness He requireth is to feel your need of Him.
I will arise and go to Jesus, He will embrace me in His arms;
In the arms of my dear Savior, O, there are ten thousand charms.

Dr. Silver shifted from one foot to the other. He gazed out beseechingly into the congregation and then moved his eyes to the floor, hands clasped in front of him. Nobody had responded to the invitation yet, and I kind of felt sorry for him. He looked forlorn. And yet, I was like a slinky, stuck between one step and the next. Why couldn't I make my feet move?

I had been thinking about accepting Jesus as my Savior for years, for my entire conscious life, actually. And lately, Dr. Silver's admonitions about hell, "where there will be weeping and gnashing of teeth, my friends," had scared me half to death. Mom often woke me up during the night, telling me to stop grinding my teeth because it sounded so terrible. Who wanted to spend eternity listening to that awful sound?

But each week, when the invitation arrived at the conclusion of the service, I hesitated. *Maybe next week.* Really, my chances were pretty good to make it another week. I was only nine years old. But, as I'd learned in Sunday school, none of us were guaranteed tomorrow. I might develop a fatal disease that would claim me within days, or there was the often-repeated example that I might walk right out of church and be hit by a truck. *You just never knew.*

Come, ye weary, heavy laden, lost and ruined by the fall;
If you tarry till you're better, you will never come at all.
I will arise and go to Jesus, He will embrace me in His arms;
In the arms of my dear Savior, O, there are ten thousand charms.

That's it! I scooted past my dad, around the edge of the pew, and made my way resolutely to the front, focusing on Dr. Silver like Peter focused on Jesus as he crossed the water, and I didn't take my eyes off of him, either.

One foot in front of the other, I thought, as I made my way to the altar. Dr. Silver greeted me with a big smile and a hearty handshake. We sat down on the front pew while I told him of my intentions. He motioned for the piano and organ to stop playing, and he stood to face the congregation, pulling me up next to him.

"Friends, it's my great joy to announce that little Susan Barnett desires to follow Jesus. And what a fitting day to do so – Pentecost Sunday!"

I smiled weakly, thinking that Pentecost sounded vaguely familiar, but hoping he wouldn't quiz me on its significance right there in front of the whole assembly.

"I'd like to invite each of you to share in congratulating Susan on this momentous decision after the service," Dr. Silver said, and indeed they did. A huge line ushered past, congratulating me with handshakes and hugs. Laura and Rhoda from my Sunday school class came up front to join me, and it was a joyous occasion. It was almost like I'd just gotten married, but without the gifts or flowers.

And yet, inside I felt the same as always. This was odd because I knew, right this very minute, the angels of heaven were rejoicing over me, the little lost lamb that had now come home. I figured I would have noticed more of a change if Jesus had saved me from a life of booze and hard living like some of the tough cases out there. Currently, my greatest transgressions were a covetous spirit toward my sister's Fisher Price Three Bears Cottage, and a low-grade desire to take dance lessons. I was just a little kid, aware of her sin and in need of a Savior.

Member after member of the faithful pumped my hand and blessed me with big bear hugs, and I felt happiness and relief wash over me. I was a Christian now, a real one, and I couldn't wait to see the adventures Jesus and I would tackle together.

Chapter 2 – God of Our Fathers

God of our fathers, whose almighty hand
Leads forth in beauty all the starry band
Of shining worlds in splendor through the skies
Our grateful songs before Thy throne arise.

In the beginning, God created the heavens and the earth.

In 1964, he created me. For three years, it was just the three of us: me, Mom, and Dad. I was happy with this arrangement, and when my sister Jill arrived, Mom recorded my reaction: *Babies just* ***bug*** *me!*

We lived in Seymour, Indiana, population 13,000. Seymour was big enough for the important things, like a movie theater and a McDonald's, but it was also small enough to have inspired John Mellencamp to immortalize it in his song "Small Town." He grew up in Seymour, too.

My dad coached Johnny "Cougar" Mellencamp on the junior high basketball team, and apparently Johnny was much more impressive later in the rock 'n' roll world than he was on the small town basketball court. Dad's great passion was sports, and he was usually an amiable presence at home, when he was indeed present.

His work as an elementary school teacher, and later, principal, resulted in many hours away. Dad ran the timer at high school basketball games as well, and when he finally arrived home, the sun was usually setting.

So it fell to Mom to direct the details of our lives, and she was up for the challenge. One night I sat with her in a PTA meeting where the adults were instructed to write their life goal on a slip of paper. I sneaked a peek at Mom's, which read *To be a good Christian wife and mother.*

She gave it her best shot. Mom trotted me to the library's story time at age three, and recorded her observation that I was ***quite*** *backward.* She also recorded *Susan sucks her two fingers a lot while pulling her hair out with her right hand. It is thin there.*

But to Mom, this was just an invitation to try harder. She heard on the radio that it was a sign of intelligence if a child could skip at an early age, and in short order she and I were standing on the back patio.

"I'm going to show you how to skip." Mom took a few loping strides down the concrete before explaining, "You just kind of run and hop at the same time."

I tilted my head, thinking about this. I could run. I could hop. But simultaneously? I gave it my best shot, but even I could tell that this was not skipping.

"Go on, go on," Mom cheered, although it was clear that my efforts were going nowhere.

"Well, Rome wasn't built in a day. We'll give it the 'ol college try again tomorrow!" she said, walking inside to start supper.

Thus my intellectual fate was predicted, and the forecast was not auspicious.

But she didn't give up, no, not my mom. "Let's get this show on the road," was a frequent rallying cry as she spurred Jill and me on to yet another project. She kept us busy with various classes and lessons, and we learned many things, not least among them the value of hard work.

And we did work hard, because we were German. Mom liked to tout our German heritage as the cause of everything from our work ethic to our stubbornness to maybe even our propensity toward varicose veins. Whenever a family member was praised or corrected for something, the typical response was a shrug and the comment, "We're German." I wasn't quite sure whether this was some type of disability or gift, although it didn't seem to qualify me for any special services.

My mom's German parents were reserved and quiet; at least my schoolteacher grandma was. My grandpa was a man with a passion for evangelism, and his eyes would light up if there were a potential convert within a stone's throw. He would go on visitation to new neighborhood residents, informally preaching to them the message of Good News and getting them to church, if it was within his power to do so.

Their house had three wonderful things: a glittering pink bead curtain that hung over the bathroom window, a breezeway connecting the house and the garage, and a decorated, fully-functional kitchen in the middle of their unfinished basement. This had been built when my great-aunt lived with them for a time, because of course you couldn't have two cooks share one kitchen.

My dad's parents were German as well, although you could have fooled me there. Mamaw was a spitfire, laughing boisterously but also putting me in my place on a regular basis.

"You girls want some cookies? I ain't got many left!" she'd yell from her kitchen.

"Mamaw," I walked over to her quietly and tugged on her sleeve, "you're not supposed to say 'ain't'."

Mamaw twisted her mouth, narrowed her eyes, and shook her spatula at me.

"Missy, I been sayin' 'ain't' all my life, and you ain't gonna stop me now. Now go an' eat a cookie!"

Duly chastened, I did. And I knew better than to correct Mamaw's word choice ever again.

Visits to their farmhouse followed a predictable pattern. Papaw walked up and swiped his hand across my face, proclaiming "Look! I got your nose!" as he proudly held up a bit of his thumb between his second and third fingers. This struck me as particularly ridiculous, as his thumb tip didn't look remotely like my nose, and anyway, why would someone greet his granddaughter by taking her nose? But I'd play along, giggling and reaching up to feel if any of my nose remained. Papaw then tilted his head, put on a sly grin, and opened up his arms. “Who’s got a little sugar for me?”

This question never failed to unnerve me a little. My own parents rarely hugged or kissed me, and the prospect of giving a little sugar to someone, even my own flesh and blood, was a bit awkward. I can still feel the stubble of Papaw’s cheek as he rubbed it against mine. Mamaw would follow up with another embrace, and it was more body contact than I’d had in a month. If it made me a little antsy, hey -- I was German.

Our German stoicism carried over to church, although perhaps the German steely-upper-lip and the Baptist church seem like odd companions. First Baptist, however, was fairly reserved. Clapping during a service was rare, and anyone raising his hands would be stared at, albeit politely, as an oddity. About the wildest thing anyone ever did was to call out “Amen!” after a moving song or a particularly cogent point in the sermon. The more outgoing the individual, the louder the “Amen” might be, and I always knew I’d scored a hit when I got a chorus of Amens after a solo. “It got a lot of Amens!” was the highest compliment a performer could receive.

***

We lived in a brand new split-level house that Dad had helped build, and one of its wonders was that I could jump the entire five-step space between one floor and another in a single leap. The house was a comforting presence: the sound of the attic fan as it circulated the humid southern Indiana air on August nights, the smell of pancakes wafting up to my room in the mornings. I could monopolize a visitor for at least ten minutes with a story about the various swirls and knots in the family room paneling. *This is an elephant -- see his eye? And here’s a river, and this is a squirrel that’s running away from the elephant ....*

We used an old washing machine, complete with a wringer, in the utility room, and it “walked” across the floor as it churned the clothes clean. Mom fed the clothes through the wringer piece by piece, *warshing* each attentively and cautioning me that one must always be careful of one’s fingers. She went on to share harrowing tales of acquaintances who had forever after been maimed due to a moment of carelessness with the wringer.

Jill and I shared a room, so that the third bedroom could be our playroom. Having this pleasant space, where we could leave out our toys all the time, was something I wished for every child.

***

It's a fact that you can get closer to heaven in a tree swing than any other way. At least, that was my theory, tested over many hours of practice.

When Dad came home with some rope and a swing seat and walked out to the big oak tree in the backyard after supper one night, I had a feeling that he was up to something good. He climbed a ladder way, way up high, to a lonely branch probably 20 feet off the ground, and went to town screwing in the parts for this wonderful swing.

Mom tested the swing first, but after she'd complete a single arc, a bolt came out and she made a quick descent to earth. Dad had to start over. So I was a little scared when my turn came to try out the swing, but I overcame my fear quickly.

That tree swing was the first place I'd run each afternoon after depositing my plastic ladybug school satchel on the kitchen table. I'd swing, and swing, and swing, loving the feel of the breeze ruffling my hair and squeezing between my barefoot toes. I'd pump higher and higher, so high that it seemed I was kin to the birds making nests up in the branches. The tree swing was worlds better than its now-ignored stepsister on the wobbly metal swing set. It even beat out the rope swing, anchored to an adjoining branch. Because there's a limit to the amount of time even a child's bottom can comfortably sway back and forth on nothing more substantial than a large knot. The tree swing was the clear winner.

As I swung, I flew over the sand box made from a tractor tire. I looked over the five acres of swaying corn behind the house. I thought about the day's events, both the good and the bad. I pondered why the teacher said to cross out two in borrowing because you can't do two take away eight, and after awhile it kind of made sense. I thought about Jesus and why he had to die for all of us, and why the bad guys had to be so awfully, awfully mean that they killed him. Couldn't they have just ignored him, or maybe put him in jail? When I was tired of thinking, I'd sing through hymns in my head, all the verses. They made a musical soundtrack for my flights of fancy, and if heaven could top this, I couldn't imagine how.

Chapter 3 – Jesus Loves the Little Children

Jesus loves the little children,
All the children of the world
Red and yellow, black and white,
They are precious in His sight.
Jesus loves the little children of the world.

I sat on the worn braided rug in Miss Fairy's Sunday school class, belting out "Jesus Loves the Little Children." I had my boisterous sing-shout voice down pat at the ripe old age of four.

If I didn't grow up actually *in* the church, like little Samuel, I did the next closest thing. Our family came to First Baptist each Sunday morning, Sunday night, and Wednesday night, and it's no wonder Mom noted that one of my earliest verbalizations was an attempt to say "Jesus" at 16 months.

My repertoire of Sunday school songs was impressive, and "I'm in the Lord's Army" was a favorite. Lest anyone doubt the educational value of such songs, this one taught me the difference between the *cavalry,* which meant riding horses in the army, and *Calvary*, which was where Jesus died. It just wouldn't do to sing about riding in the *Calvary*, and I was half-tempted to point this out to people when I heard them make the unfortunate substitution.

I may never march in the infantry
Ride in the cavalry
Shoot the artillery
I may never fly o'er the enemy
But I'm in the Lord's army!

"Okay, boys and girls, 'Only a Boy Named David'," Miss Fairy told us. I loved this one because of the enthusiastic motions. Miss Fairy led us in circling our imaginary slings round and round, and I was so fascinated watching the excess flesh on her arm jiggle that I forgot all about David's heroics.

And round and round, and round, and round, and round, and round, and round.
And one little stone went up in the air, and the giant came tumbling down.

But it didn't matter, because there would always be another telling (or singing) of David's story, as well as of Abraham's, and Joseph's, and of course Jesus'.

***

I was just fine with singing songs on the rug in Sunday school class. But when Miss Fairy announced that we were going to *perform in the big church, for all our parents,* well, I wasn't so sure about that. After all, I was *quite backward*, and when I spied the risers in the front of the sanctuary, I wanted no part of them.

Mom had enough confidence for both of us.

"Susan, you're a big girl! You are four years old! You just walk up onto those risers like they're stairs here at home, and then you look out into the audience and you sing! I think you'll do just great," she said, nodding her head and smiling confidently. I wasn't so sure, but how could I let her down when she had such faith in me? The night of the 4's and 5's performance, I bravely ascended the steps and stood next to my friend Tommy.

We immediately began peeking back into the three-foot drop-off behind us, which looked to me like the Grand Canyon I'd seen in the World Book Encyclopedia. I enjoyed swaying back and forth over the edge of the risers more than singing, and sure enough, a few minutes later Tommy and I both tumbled into the abyss.

A helper quickly returned us to our spots, just in time for "Zacchaeus Was a Wee Little Man."

Zacchaeus was a wee little man, a wee little man was he …

I wasn't sure just how *wee* Zacchaeus actually was, but judging from my hand motions, he was about five inches tall. I imagined the challenges he might have faced in climbing that sycamore, and the utter fear he must have felt when Jesus cornered him, up in that tree.

And He said, "Zacchaeus, you come down! For I'm going to your house today."

I wondered, exactly how did Jesus say the words to him? What tone of voice was he using? Because I knew that tone was everything.

But my time to reflect was limited, because we were moving on to "This Little Light of Mine."

This little light of mine, I'm gonna let it shine
This little light of mine, I'm gonna let it shine
This little light of mine, I'm gonna let it shine
Let it shine, Let it shine, Let it shine.

Hide it under a bushel? No! I'm gonna let it shine
Hide it under a bushel? No! I'm gonna let it shine
Hide it under a bushel? No! I'm gonna let it shine
Let it shine, Let it shine, Let it shine.

Don't let Satan blow it out, I'm gonna let it shine
Don't let Satan blow it out, I'm gonna let it shine
Don't let Satan blow it out, I'm gonna let it shine
Let it shine, Let it shine, Let it shine.

Next to me, Sammy proudly shone his light. He was using his middle finger, which didn't look quite right. There was some quiet chuckling from the congregation, but I knew that was just because they really liked us. I shone my index finger and sang with gusto.

***

Hearing stories in Miss Fairy's class was even better than singing. And the highlight of any story was its flannelgraph illustrations. Jesus, the disciples, the patriarchs, and various animals paraded in turn across the flannel background, and I came to know them all as friends. When Mom taught Sunday school, I sometimes helped her prepare her flannelgraph characters for the lesson. I learned why the disciples were usually depicted as one large flannel group -- it was too time-consuming to punch out all twelve individually.

Flannelgraph animals had the unfortunate tendency to lose their thin limbs. After a story had been told a time or two, any sheep still in possession of all four legs was a rarity. Those who were still intact often had badly creased legs, which I'd shore up by gluing popsicle sticks to the back.

But even with these defects, flannelgraph stories had the ability to capture a tale and sear it into my mind. Forever after, I pictured Jesus wearing a white tunic with a royal blue sash draped diagonally across his chest. He had a beard, and honey-brown hair with golden highlights. I knew this beyond the shadow of a doubt.

"You know, we really don't know what Jesus looked like, since there were no cameras then," Mom casually mentioned one day as I was drying dishes at the sink while she washed.

I was momentarily stunned, because this revelation rocked my world. I couldn't deny the truth that cameras had not existed BC.

"But … why do the pictures always show him with brown hair?"

Mom kept washing. "Oh, I guess because that's how most people looked in that part of the world at that time."

I didn't see this as a very compelling answer. What if Jesus had actually had *blonde* hair? This would change my whole impression of him! What if Jesus had brown skin? What if he, heaven forbid, was Asian? Suddenly, my whole idea of Jesus was in jeopardy, and I didn't like the feeling one bit.

"I wouldn't spend too much time worrying about it." Mom closed the conversation as she pulled the stopper out of the drain.

But I most certainly did, because Jesus was my best friend. How could I have a best friend who I couldn't visualize?

Chapter 4 – The Little Brown Church in the Vale

There's a church in the valley by the wildwood
no lovelier place in the dale
No spot is so dear to my childhood
than the little brown church in the vale

Some kids dream of traveling to Narnia or Oz, but I felt no need for that: I had the First Baptist Church to explore.

First Baptist Church in Seymour, Indiana, where I grew up, dated back to 1839. That is when "ten praying members," meeting in the woods, founded Liberty Baptist Church.

I have all the respect in the world for those hearty folks, who apparently met in the wilderness for twenty years before constructing a church building in the nearby town of Seymour in 1859. Seymour Hospital, where I was born, now stands at the site of that church.

The congregation put up a new brick church close by in 1885, and it remained until 1966, when the church I knew was built. I was just a year old, but if I close my eyes and go back to my earliest, foggiest memories, I can see the stained glass and the big wooden front doors of the old church. I can remember how it felt to be carried up the steps leading to the big sanctuary.

But the new First Baptist was the church I would come to know and love. Its halls and walls, rooms and secret niches, became as familiar to me as the story of Jesus.

During the many hours spent sitting in the sanctuary, I had hour upon hour to study its architecture and design. The walls behind the altar were made of multi-color brick, which offered all kinds of diversions for anyone with an imagination. I could count how many dark brown bricks there were. How many light brown? How many gray? Were there any patterns in the bricks?

Over the baptistry stood a stained glass window, which provided more mental stimulation. How many pieces of glass made up the butterfly's left wing? Were there the same number of pieces in the right wing? It hurt my head, trying to remember the first set of numbers while I counted the second. My first grade teacher should be grateful for that window, because it taught me so much math. I'd count the pieces in each section and think *odd* or *even.* There were a lot of sections, so I got to be really good at it.

Stained glass windows lined the sides of the sanctuary as well, but in keeping with the church's 1960s design, these windows didn't depict Biblical scenes. Instead, their focal point looked more like a boomerang, or maybe a duck's bent wing if you thought about it, which I certainly had the time to do. When an usher flipped on the hallway lights, they would shine through these windows and I knew that the end of the service must be near.

The actual humans in the sanctuary were even more fascinating to study than the architecture. Who was missing today from the choir loft behind the pastor? Had Mrs. Blevins gotten a new haircut? Who was the newcomer next to Mr. Kidwell? Occasionally, a choir member would make eye contact with me while I checked them out, and I found this highly embarrassing. Jill, on the other hand, loved staring down choir members, and made a game out of counting those she could conquer.

My parents, sister and I always sat in the second pew on the left. This premium spot was due to Mom being church pianist and needing a seat close to the piano. It had its benefits, as we could make easy entrances and exits, as well as observe all the congregants as they arrived. Dad and I livened up many a dull moment there, playing the hand game. I pulled out a hymnal and put it onto my lap, and put my hand down on top of it. Dad put his hand on mine, I put my other hand on top of his, and when we ran out of hands we'd start pulling hands from the bottom of the stack, faster and faster, until it was all we could do to keep our laughter quiet as we slapped at each other playfully.

First Baptist was a large, sprawling place, even more so to a six year old. Its long, long hallway had a steep incline that was ideal for running. Or it would have been, had my parents not taught me that it was not proper to run in God's house. So I fought the urge with each trip down that hall -- although I did walk fast on more than a few occasions.

The nursery stood at one end of the hallway, and I loved looking through its big window at all the cute babies and toddlers. When Mom came to church for a meeting and brought Jill and me along, we often ended up in the nursery, studying the framed painting on the wall. It showed a gigantic angel who looked similar to how I pictured Mary Ingalls. She had gigantic feathery wings, and her face glowed as she benevolently raised her hands over a little boy and girl in front of her. The boy and girl, whom I'd dubbed Hansel and Gretel, were walking over a bridge, and if you looked carefully you saw why they needed the angel. A big board was missing from the bridge, which was spanning a waterfall-laden rushing river. This painting gave me a perfect picture of guardian angels, and I loved its serenity and mystery.

Sunday school classrooms lined the rest of the hallway, each boasting a printed nameplate above the door. We had the Friendship Class and the ubiquitous Berean Class (they studied the scriptures daily). But First Baptist also had a few classes with utterly puzzling monikers: the Amoma Class. The Agoga Class. The Crusaders. The Loyal Daughters. These names were always a source of wonderment as I walked past the classrooms, which seemed to be filled with impossibly-old people.

Down the hallway was a turn to yet another long corridor, which ended with the fellowship center. Fellowship Hall was a wonderful place, with a large stage. It also doubled as a venue for church suppers and wedding receptions, and it was lined with classrooms for the teens. Exploring the nooks and crannies of Fellowship Hall was a real treat, and I am convinced that the Paris Opera House had nothing on the backstage area at First Baptist. There were all manner of unexplainable side rooms and closets, and we strove mightily to open and close the massive velvet stage curtains. If the Phantom of the Opera himself had appeared to me there, I would have almost expected him.

But some of the places most vivid in my memories are the most humble. One of my favorite spots was a particular stall in one of the many bathrooms. How many minutes did I spend sitting on a toilet there, staring out through the crack between the stall door and the wall and wondering whether people could see me as easily as I could see them. Looking up, I smiled at two children-of-the-world stickers stuck on the back of the stall door. They'd been there for as long as I could remember: the pigtailed face of a Dutch girl and the disembodied head of a Chinese boy. Who had put them there? And just how strong was their adhesive, since apparently no janitor had ever been able to remove them? I wondered about this every time I gazed at them, which was often.

I even was familiar with the hardware on the stall door, which I had decided resembled an elephant head. The piece that protruded into the door itself was the trunk.

How could one small space hold so many wonders? I was sure that Neverland itself could offer nothing better.

***

I couldn't imagine First Baptist without Dr. Silver, and I couldn't imagine Dr. Silver without First Baptist. He arrived there the year prior to my birth, and he was there when I grew up and left.

Miraculously, from the time I first knew him until I graduated from high school, Dr. Silver remained permanently somewhere between 55 and 60. His hair was shiny and dark, flecked with silver, and it looked like it would crunch if you touched it, which of course you wouldn't. He usually had a slight smile on his face and a twinkle in his eye, yet you wouldn't dream of running up to him with a knock-knock joke

I knew many things about Dr. Silver. His favorite book was Revelation, and he liked the word carnal. He also liked to call us beloved, with the word drawn out the full three syllables. His favorite invitation hymn was "Just As I Am," which we sang approximately every other Sunday for the altar call. He liked wearing suits, or if he didn't he could have fooled me, since I don't know if I ever saw him in anything else. One year, the Christmas *Messenger* arrived in our mailbox, featuring photos of all the church staff and their families. Dr. Silver was pictured in a sweater vest, and I had to stare at the photo for ten minutes to be sure it was really him. Dr. Silver in a sweater (or, heaven forbid, a leisure suit) was like John the Baptist in bellbottoms -- unimaginable.

I figured Dr. Silver was a lot like God would be, if God were a person. You knew him, but then again, you really didn't. I had no idea what Dr. Silver's favorite color was, or his favorite kind of cookie, or his favorite TV show, if he even watched TV.

Chapter 5 – Be Ye Kind

Be ye kind, be ye kind, be ye kind to one another,
Be ye kind, be ye kind, be ye kind to one another!

I stepped out of the plastic pool and put my hands on my hips. With as much exasperation as a four year old could muster, I shouted, "Tommy! Don't cha remember? Be ye kind!"

Tommy had just splashed me, and I found this perplexing. Hadn't we just sat in Miss Fairy's class a couple of hours ago? Hadn't we just sung "Be Ye Kind?" Hadn't we discussed what that meant? So why was he now splashing me? I was confused and annoyed, but mostly annoyed.

Tommy's mom and my mom were best friends, and so Tommy and I were best friends by default rather than by choice. When Tommy's family moved, Mom faced a crisis: where would she find a new friend for me? My world was small, revolving around toys, TV shows, and weekly trips to our neighbor Mrs. Koester's house, where Mom and I would "visit." Visiting Mrs. Koester was the height of excitement to me, because her house was so different from ours. Mr. Koester had long since gone on to his reward, and Mrs. Koester was old as the hills. She lived with a little indoor dog named Tippy who had so much energy he scared the daylights out of me as he zipped around the quiet house. Mrs. Koester had doilies on the back of each chair in her living room, where your head would go, and this was both lovely and puzzling. What was the point of the doily? Was it only decorative, or was it also a type of makeshift pillow for one to lean back on, if one should fall asleep while visiting?

Mrs. Koester and Mom visited, each sitting in a living room chair and talking about non-objectionable topics for an hour or so: *This humidity is sure working for the corn, I've never seen it this high in June! My heavens, did you see the wreck yesterday on South Walnut? The Robbins' irises are the prettiest color this year!* and so forth.

I sat in my own chair, quietly so as not to risk breaking one of the hundreds of little knickknacks sitting around. Tiny china dogs were abundant, as were delicate glass dishes. Mrs. Koester's whole house seemed so breakable that I feared for it with Tippy inside.

My only other outings involved occasional trips to story time at the library. However, chanting "Teddy bear, teddy bear, turn around!" and listening to Mrs. Graves read *Green Eggs and Ham* wasn't much of a social experience. For me, there was not found a companion suitable. And so, Mom turned to church.

***

"Susan, come down here. We're going to visit the Cordeses. They just adopted a little Indian girl, and she's about your age!"

This did have potential for excitement. I'd never seen a real Indian before, and I hoped Rhoda would be wearing a headdress and perhaps even a doll papoose on her back.

But once we had arrived, I was dismayed to find that Rhoda looked similar to me, although she did have black hair and her skin was slightly darker. We sized each other up shyly as our moms visited, with Rhoda giggling intermittently. This put me on edge because I wasn't sure if she was laughing at me or with me, but since I wasn't laughing I had to assume the former. We failed to forge much of a connection.

Mom and I went calling on other potential friends. Melissa's family was new to our church, and since she was a year older, she intimidated me from the moment I walked through the door.

While our moms enjoyed their visit, Melissa and I put on a show. Or more accurately, I should say Melissa put on a show while I watched. She sauntered down the open staircase in what I thought was a very mature way, lip synching "Go Away, Little Girl" into a hairbrush microphone. My job was to re-start the record each time it ended, and I did this over and over and over again. I was mighty impressed with Melissa's confidence, and sensed that she was way too self-assured for me.

***

"Mom, if I died tonight would I go to heaven?" This thought had occurred to me as I spread deviled ham on crackers, and the answer seemed awfully important.

"Well, you need to accept Jesus as your Savior. That's how you become a Christian."

"I know, but if a baby dies, he goes to heaven even though he didn't ask Jesus, right, because a baby doesn't know to ask?"

"Well, right."

"But when does someone go from automatically going to heaven, to having to accept Jesus as their Savior?"

"I'm not totally sure on that. Really, I think it's different for each person." Mom walked outside to get some onions from the garden, and I noticed that she seemed a little relieved to be going.

I furrowed my brow. It appeared that some questions stumped even adults.

***

I grew up with a nebulous concept called the age of accountability. Before this age, babies and little kids got a free pass into heaven. But once you'd reached the age of accountability, the age when you knew right from wrong, you had to ask Jesus to forgive your sins. I thought about this concept a lot, and I thought that it made some sense intuitively, but I needed details. I was seven -- had I reached that age yet? I did know right from wrong, and I thought about God an awful lot, so I guessed I had. And yet, it seemed unfair that some people reached that age before others. Why should someone morally clueless get extra months or even years of get-into-heaven-free time? I didn't like that.

At First Baptist, the blanket age of accountability was presumed to be first grade. At least, that's when Sunday school began dividing into separate classes for boys and girls.

My class of girls became my universe for the next decade. It was filled with girls red and yellow, black and white; girls who were quiet and unnoticed along with girls who were mouthy and impossible to miss. We were a wildly disparate group who would never have befriended each other in the real world, yet in church all things were possible, so here we were.

***

"Class, meet Laura. Her family just moved to town and we're so happy to have her in our Sunday school class!" Miss Harrington enthused.

I eyed Laura curiously. I was favorably disposed to her just on the basis of her name, since I loved the Little House on the Prairie books. But I soon learned that this Laura was as far from the Half Pint of the Prairie as Wilma Flintstone was from Judy Jetson.

Laura was a tomboy, and she forged an immediate bond with Rhoda. Together, they drew mustaches on the disciples in the Bible storybook while Miss Harrington prayed, and they played catch with their Bibles before she arrived at class. I watched all this wide-eyed, for I was in their world, but not of it.

***

Then there was Bekki, the third in a family of four girls. The oldest sister got all the sweetness and goodness, the second all the leadership skills, and by the time Bekki came along all that was left was an abundance of attitude and a desire to constantly chew gum. Bekki's mom Rose lived up to her name, always smiling as she hustled her short, plump form after her girls and husband.

Bekki hosted some great birthday parties, and during one of them Rose entered the living room with a mysterious look on her face and her hands behind her back.

"Okay, girls, now it's time for games!"

My stomach tightened at the mention of games, because birthday party games were not my favorite activity, especially if they involved running, jumping, or other large motor skills, which they usually did. My most unfavorite birthday party game was unfortunately quite popular at Seymour parties. Two guests each grabbed balloons and raced to chairs, where they attempted to pop their balloons as fast as they could by sitting on them. The idea of popping a balloon with my bottom horrified me for several reasons: the noise, the possible backfiring of the rubber, and a whole host of other unknowns. So every time this game was announced, my first act was to ask to go to the bathroom, where I'd stay until I heard the game end.

I steeled myself for an announcement of The Balloon Game, but instead Rose pulled her hands out in front of her. She was holding the most wondrous thing. It was a little Kiddle doll. Jill and I had many Kiddle dolls. Mom kept them in a small suitcase that she took down from the closet shelf for us to play with when we'd been good. We had Kiddles with dresses, Kiddles with pants (which were very hard to take on and off), and even a Kiddle with a sailor suit.

But this Kiddle was unlike any I'd ever seen. She was wearing a little lion suit, and every morsel of her two-inch height captivated me. She had tiny felt lion ears and a mane made of orange yarn, and as I stared into her big, blue eyes, I knew that fate had brought us together.

"Here's the prize for our first game!" Rose said, smiling as usual, and I could tell as she looked around at our reactions that she recognized just how neat a prize this was. I braced myself to pop five balloons with my bottom, if necessary, in order to win that Kiddle.

Mercifully, I didn't have to, because the game involved Rose carrying around a tray full of objects for us all to look at. After a minute, she took the tray away and we had to write down everything we could remember. I focused on that tray like a man on death row must have zeroed in on his last supper.

Barbie shoe ... eraser shaped like an elephant ... love beads ... stick of gum ...

My powers of concentration were so great that I remembered every item on the tray, and when Rose handed me the lion Kiddle, I couldn't have been more proud if she'd crowned me Miss America.

"That's a very cool Kiddle," Bekki said to me, popping her gum, and I could only nod in awed agreement.

As Mom drove me home later, I pressed my legs into the warm vinyl car seat and stared at my Kiddle, balancing delicately on my knees. I knew that I led a blessed life.

***

It was an irony of my childhood that most of my friends came not from church, but from school. This bothered me, knowing that Christians weren't to be "unequally yoked," but I was hoping that the verse referred more to marriage than to friendship.

"I like your lunchbox," I said shyly to the new girl standing under the massive sycamore tree in the schoolyard at recess.

She looked down at her lunchbox, and then up at me, and smiled.

"Thanks." Opening the lunchbox, she opened a double pack of Ho Hos and gave one to me.

From this simple beginning, my years-long friendship with Miriam began. We were both in first grade, and the first thing that attracted me was that wonderful lunchbox. It was shaped like a school bus, with various Disney characters cavorting along its sides. It was the lunchbox I'd always wanted. My mom had won a perfectly fine Disney World lunchbox in a contest, and she'd given it to me for Christmas. But it wasn't the school bus. It didn't have a curved top, into which the thermos fit like a glove.

And so Miriam and I began a childhood friendship, appropriately, over food. Appropriately, because Miriam and I shared two major traits: we were good, smart girls, and we were chubby. Neither turned out to be an advantage.

Chapter 6 – Lord, Speak to Me

O teach me, Lord, that I may teach
The precious things Thou dost impart;
And wing my words, that they may reach
The hidden depths of many a heart.

I couldn't wait to learn to read. But I was out of luck until I reached first grade, because Mom wouldn't teach me. She feared that her lack of teaching knowledge would damage me permanently as a reader, and thus I could only stare at the letters wistfully until Miss Wilson taught me in a proper way. This same theory banned me from early typing on the typewriter, and I felt the loss keenly.

In kindergarten, I'd memorized *The Rabbit Ran* and performed the book for the class, but memorizing wasn't true reading, so I figured it didn't really count.

So on the August day when I was called back to the Sunflowers reading group and taught the words "Janet" and "Mark,"

I was ecstatic. The next day, we learned "Janet *and* Mark." My excitement knew no bounds, and I was off and running, reading everything I could get my hands on.

Miss Wilson appreciated this, and asked for my assistance in helping the Blue Violets, which was the dumb reading group, when I finished my morning worksheets. I happily obliged. Tutoring was much more interesting than cutting and pasting ten words that rhymed with *at*.

***

I took to learning like Eve to the apple. There were so many fascinating things in the world! I was particularly enthralled with social studies, and I wanted to see Machu Picchu so badly that I could almost taste it. Those high peaks set against the blue, blue sky fueled my imagination and drove home the fact that the world consisted of more than fields of soybeans.

We studied atolls, and I found them so wonderful that I wasn't content to just read the chapter and answer the questions at the end. Mrs. Baughman was forever encouraging us to create visual aids for the reports she assigned, and I went a little overboard on these. I wanted to make visual aids for almost everything we studied. I wanted to create an atoll! So, I dug out some construction paper and created a mosaic picture of one. Then, I taped blue tissue paper over the bottom half so that the base of the atoll appeared to be underwater. I regarded this as one of my coolest bits of artwork ever, and Mom insisted, "You need to show that to Mrs. Baughman."

And so I did, but she just glanced at it before saying, "That's nice, dear," and moving on to the next kid in line at her desk. I wasn't discouraged, though, because I hadn't made it for her, anyway. There was a big world out there, and I wanted to explore every bit of it.

***

Mrs. Baughman wrote on the board:

Social Studies, pages 168-170: Europe

I knew all about Europe. That was where Germany was, the home of our ancestors. Mom loved family history; it was one of her favorite hobbies next to making broomstick lace. I'd spent many hours sitting at her feet in the library as she scrolled through the microfilm and microfiche reels, looking for that bit of the 1860 census that could tell her where Philip Gerdemann went after leaving Cincinnati.

"Mom?"

Scroll, scroll, scroll. "What?"

"Are you ever gonna go to Germany?"

Mom stopped scrolling and looked down at me. "Actually *go* there? Oh, I doubt that."

"Why not? You're always reading about it."

"To get to Germany, I'd have to get on a plane, and I'm scared to do that. So, no." She returned her attention to the screen.

I thought. "Well, when I grow up you can go to Germany with me. Maybe we can go on a boat." It was so easy, solving life's little problems.

"We'll see about that." Scroll, click click.

But today, as I stared at the word Europe on the board, a wonderful thing happened. Mrs. Baughman said it aloud, "Europe," and I realized that this was Your-Up. When I'd read that word in books, I'd always dismissed it as Ee-ah-rope, a magical land the whereabouts of which I had no idea.

You mean to tell me Europe and Ee-ah-rope were the same place? My mind boggled. This was kind of like the time I realized that euthanasia had nothing to do with Chinese kids. It was a revelation, a moment when the key slid smoothly and perfectly into the doorknob.

***

Telling time did me in.

I understood the o'clocks and the half pasts just fine, but everything else was a mystery. Mom bought a little book with a clock face and plastic hands, and Dad spent hours trying to teach me the difference between 7:10 and 8:40.

"See," he'd begin patiently, "when the big hand is straight up, it's o'clock. But when the big hand is on the one, it's five after."

"But if the big hand is on the one, why isn't it one after?" This made no sense to me, and I didn't like the feeling one bit.

"Those numbers count by fives. The one is five, the two is ten, and so on. So," he arranged the clock to read 4:35, "what time is it now?"

"Four seven?"

Dad shook his head. "No, now I just told you, you have to count by fives."

"Twenty thirty-five?"

Dad rubbed his neck and sighed. He was a teacher by profession, but I had observed that teachers generally worked best with kids who didn't need a lot of instruction.

During second grade, I spent a humiliating few weeks getting back one math worksheet after another with Mrs. Gebhart's beautiful, flowing cursive U written on the top. We got U, for unsatisfactory, until third grade, when we were deemed old enough to handle the harsher F.

I turned around and caught Christina methodically cutting a U off of her paper. Looking at her desk, she was apparently struggling with more than just telling time. There was a whole stack of U's.

"Christina," I asked, "even if you cut off the U, isn't your mom gonna notice that? Won't she still see the ones you got wrong? Won't she see the holes in your papers?"

Christina looked at me, shrugged, and cut off another U. Some things were just mysteries.

***

As embarrassed as I was by my poor showing in time-telling, I knew better than to try to pull a fast one by cutting grades off my papers. Because teachers weren't known for their leniency when it came to misbehavior. When Brian got bored from cutting and pasting short-a words and decided to cut off his bangs instead, Miss Wilson taped them back. He had to walk around school all day with the humiliating results of his actions plastered across his forehead.

And as we got older, the punishments were even harsher. In fifth grade, Tonda made an uncalled-for remark and Mr. Hulfachor marched her right out into the hall, where he paddled her. The rest of us were quiet as death, listening to each fall of the board as it landed on Tonda's behind. To her credit, she cried out only once.

We didn't have counselors to commiserate with our hardships, and sometimes the teacher wrote MESSY! on papers that really weren't that awful.

But when recess time arrived, we all ran outside and played tag, and jumped rope, and searched for four leaf clovers, and Missy Lukemeyer proved how much she loved horses by actually eating grass. The sun shone down on us, and it was glorious just to be alive.

Chapter 7 – He's Got the Whole World in His Hands

He's got you & me sister in his hands,
He's got you & me sister in his hands,
He's got you & me sister in his hands,
He's got the whole world in his hands!

If I could distill my entire childhood into one happy afternoon, it would be spent in the playhouse.

The summer I was seven, Dad built Jill and me a playhouse in the backyard. Dad often took construction jobs in the summer since he was off from teaching, and he put his carpenter skills to use in creating the most fabulous playhouse I could imagine.

Jill and I eagerly watched as he poured the concrete slab, and then the playhouse itself began to go up. It had a front porch perfect for sitting on Indian-style, devouring ice cream swirl cups that tasted like the wooden sticks we used to eat them. The playhouse had two windows and carpet inside. A woodpecker doorknocker hung next to the door. It was heaven on earth.

Struggling to find a worthy use for such a spot, Jill and I began by forming the Spooky Spy Club, which met in the playhouse.

We hung a large plastic spider so that it dangled from the ceiling, and we invited friends over to club meetings where we'd pledge allegiance to the spider. The Spooky Spy Club had a short-lived and mostly uneventful history, although once, in the spirit of spookiness, Beth Noblitt swore that while on the way to a meeting, she closed her eyes for a moment and when she opened them, she had been magically transported instantaneously to the playhouse porch. We reflected endlessly on how this truly spooky thing had happened, but no one was ever able to offer a plausible explanation.

Mom thought the playhouse could use a little more sprucing up, so she sewed calico curtains for the windows and brought in a second-hand child's stove and sink, but I'm afraid we crushed her intentions for domestic play.

Because when I saw the playhouse, I didn't dream of playing with dolls and mixing up pretend suppers. I dreamed of an entire world for my kids.

Jill and I had almost a hundred "kids," which was the name we gave our vast collection of Fisher Price Little People. We loved them as Jesus must have loved the missing sheep. We knew each one by name, and we named them for various people we knew in real life. Cousins, friends, and favorite teachers were all likely to show up as two-inch facsimiles in our kid town.

The stories of our devotion to our kids were legendary within the family. A vacation to Florida was almost ruined when my Fisher Price dog, which was touted to float, drowned in the motel pool. Although the staff dutifully drained the pool in search of Toto, he never surfaced. God bless the folks at Fisher Price, who sent a replacement after Mom mailed them a letter chronicling this sad tale. The day the new Toto arrived in a padded envelope rivaled Christmas.

And probably the best Christmas of my life was the one when I was gifted the Little People Castle, and Jill received the A-Frame. The details captivated us, allowing us to vicariously live lives other than our own: the A-frame's tiny sliding glass door! Its bunk beds, complete with foam mattresses! The castle's side den where a pink and turquoise dragon lived! The castle dungeon, where naughty kids ended up spending a dreary afternoon.

We arranged an entire kid village in our playroom, but the idea of moving our world out to the playhouse was so irresistible that it gave me goosebumps in July.

So, Jill and I rolled up our sleeves, opened the door of the play stove, and began converting its shelves into a two-story city county building.

The center of the kids' world was, of course, the church. We created a huge and detailed place of worship, modeled on First Baptist. An empty Kleenex box turned on its side became the fellowship center stage, and communion cups made perfect seats. Upside-down nut cups were scale-model-perfect tables, and alphabet blocks spelled GOD LOVES YOU down a long hallway.

Our kids went to church at the same frequency we did, or maybe even more. We created tiny choir robes from fabric scraps and taped them onto the kids, and Jill was an expert as she voiced the miniature Dr. Silver: "Sleepers, awake!" (shouted with enthusiasm), or "Oh, beloved …" (this was a clear signal that the message was nearing an end).

We enjoyed our kid town out in the playhouse from the first March weekend above freezing until the final October day when we could stand it. In between, we spent many blissful hours there, kneeling on the floor with our legs sticking together in the heat. A box fan by the screen door blew around the humid air. There was a constant hum of activity as a village of carpenter bees discovered the porch rafters and refused to leave, despite my dad's best efforts to rid the playhouse of this pestilence.

Around the edges of our village, we arranged our Fisher Price School, Farm, Village, A-Frame, Houseboat, Castle, and Hospital. The hospital was especially prized because of its story. One summer, Mom offered Jill and me a choice: would we like to take a family vacation, or get the Little People Hospital? It took us about ten seconds to choose the hospital, complete with an X-ray machine, operating table, and working elevator. No trip to the beach could compare!

To fill in gaps, we created houses for our families from boxes decorated with wallpaper scraps and furniture made from Jello boxes. Furnishing our town kept us busy for many a summer day, and we relished every minute.

Our kids had recreation other than church. We set a trio of kids on the turntable of our portable record player, and when we turned it on, voila -- a perfect skating rink! We learned that using the faster speeds was a public health hazard as it resulting in kids flying off, and we never were able to find a way for the kids to skate while a record actually played, because the moving needle got in the way. Nevertheless, we loved our invention.

When the kids weren't skating, we made full use of the record player to play singles Mom picked up at garage sales.

"Here you go, girls," she said one morning, walking in through the playhouse door and handing us a new 45. "I really wanted to get you "Itsy Bitsy Teenie Weenie Yellow Polka Dot Bikini," but then I wasn't sure it was totally appropriate."

Instead, we got "Devil or Angel" and "Dream a Little Dream of Me," which I'm glad were deemed appropriate, because over the years we committed every word to memory.

***

If the playhouse seemed perfect to us, we weren't the only ones who thought so. Every child who visited was destined to wander in, giving Jill and me heart palpitations.

"The Johnsons are coming over this afternoon, so you girls make sure you are nice to Kara," Mom casually mentioned one day at lunch. My eyes met Jill's and I stopped chewing, my baloney and cheese roll-up suddenly losing its scrumptiousness. My stomach did a pretzel twist. Kara was four years old. The odds of her not noticing the playhouse ranked somewhere between slim and none.

"Does she have to go into the playhouse?" Jill asked.

Mom spun around, turning Paul Harvey's volume down on the radio.

"Now girls. Kara's no more than knee-high to a grasshopper. If you went to someone's house and they had a playhouse, wouldn't you want to go in? Maybe the place will be a little cattywampus when she leaves, but so what? Just be nice to her."

So it was settled. We figured since the enemy was coming to us, we might as well meet her on our own turf. We headed back to the playhouse and resumed the church service we'd interrupted for lunch.

***

"Wow!" Kara stood in the playhouse doorway, totally obliterating the sun.

"Yeah, it's neat, isn't it," I said, more as a statement than a question. I was hoping to show some authority here. "You can look at it, and then maybe we can go play outside …"

But my hopes ended as Kara laughed and with a single kick, wiped out the fellowship center.

"Kara!" Jill cried, horrified, "You can't just do that!"

But Kara was on a roll. She walked around the village, indiscriminately kicking down this building and that, like a human tornado. Jill and I stood by, paralyzed in our horror. We were supposed to be nice to her, and I didn't think dragging her forcefully out onto the porch counted as "nice."

After the longest minute or two we'd known in our brief lives, Kara tired of this and wandered outside, presumably to wreak havoc on the great outdoors.

***

That evening, Jill and I began the arduous task of reconstructing our town. No natural disaster was ever met with greater resolve, and within an hour we had restored Kid Town to its former glory -- or, possibly, even improved it. After all, I'd been considering some upgrades to the choir loft, and Jill had a few ideas for a new slogan to spell out along the hallway. GOD LOVES YOU was *so* 1972.

We made solemn announcements to the residents, informing them that a great danger had passed, and that it was safe to again begin their daily routines.

It wasn't so bad, having a whole world in our hands.

Chapter 8 – More About Jesus

More about Jesus would I know,
More of His grace to others show;
More of His saving fullness see,
More of His love Who died for me.
More, more about Jesus,
More, more about Jesus;
More of His saving fullness see,
More of His love Who died for me.

I sat on my chair in the third grade girls' Sunday school class, the metal cool against my bare legs. Miss Harrington, our teacher, was as old as Methuselah. I knew, from reading *The Messenger,* that she collected canceled postage stamps for the Women's Missionary Society – something I felt only an incredibly aged person would take the trouble to do. She looked like the perfect Sunday school teacher, with her floral dresses, horn-rimmed glasses and perpetual smile. When she asked me to play hymns for the class to sing on the ancient clunker of a piano in the room, I happily said yes, because that removed me from the anemic singing pool.

But the greatest thing Miss Harrington did was to offer prizes for learning Bible verses. Miss Harrington was no slacker. She awarded no points for spouting John 3:16 or "Jesus wept" each week, no siree. She made a list of the things we were required to memorize, and I took this as seriously as I did most everything else in my life.

One of the prizes I earned was a large picture of Jesus' head, which hung on my bedroom wall for years. I wondered if his eyes would follow me no matter where I went in the room, because I had read that this could happen with certain pictures. But although I tested the painting many times, I was disappointed to find Jesus' gaze never wavered from its fixed point.

"Class, I have some new prizes to show you today," Miss Harrington announced. I immediately sat up straighter as she pulled a little bag out of her purse.

"I have this stone ring, and here's a necklace with a stone, and I have a stone bracelet too. The first girl to memorize Psalms 23, 121, and 139 can choose which she wants. The second girl to do that can choose next, and the third girl will get the remaining piece. I think these are really special prizes, don't you?"

Oh, my. Did I ever! The ring and the necklace I could live without, but that bracelet! I hadn't seen such a thing of beauty since the lion Kiddle at Bekki's party. Each bracelet link alternated with a little (undoubtedly real) gold square, which held a small stone. The stones were polished, and they were different colors, and oh, I didn't actually know how I could even go home from church that day without that bracelet on my arm. I stared at the little bauble and I understood truly what it meant to covet.

I devoted every spare moment in the coming weeks to memorizing Psalms. The small fear that someone else would beat me to the bracelet nagged at me sometimes, but I figured this wasn't too likely.

I burst into Sunday school for the next three weeks with the enthusiasm of the believers after Pentecost, asking right at the start of class if I could recite my Psalm for the day. Miss Harrington happily obliged, and the day I walked out of class with the bracelet gracing my wrist was one for the record books. I smiled down at the delectable concoction of gold and shiny stones, and I knew what total happiness felt like.

***

Considering the sheer number of hours I spent listening to him, you would think I'd remember all kinds of topics Dr. Silver preached on. But, I don't. A child can only hear "Oh, brethren" so many times before it takes on an almost hypnotic power. I was paying all manner of attention - just to other things.

I always snagged *The Messenger,* First Baptist's newsletter, on my way into the sanctuary. *The Messenger* provided me with hours of reading material, listing new babies (*THE VERY NEWEST*), marriages (*WEDDING BELLS*), and illnesses (*OUR KNOWN SICK*). I always wondered about *our known sick.* Did this mean only the sick people in our own church (emphasis on OUR), or did it mean only the sick people that we knew about (emphasis on KNOWN)? The difference was subtle, but I felt it might be important. I also checked out the bus ministry driver for the week (easy, because it was always Mr. Kirk), and then deacon of the week. The deacon of the week was a high honor; I knew this because Dad had done it a time or two. The chosen deacon walked into the sanctuary at the beginning of the Sunday morning service just behind Dr. Silver, and he sat up on the podium on a special bench before offering a prayer during the service. It was fame on the level of providing special music, but being deacon of the week was even better because it didn't require singing a solo.

I merely skimmed *OUR CHRISTIAN LOVE AND SYMPATHY*, because everyone who died was most likely a member of the *SHUT-IN OF THE WEEK* list, so old that I didn't know him or her anyway. Mortality was a vague concept, although it entered my mind occasionally. I sometimes peeked into the window of an older kids' Sunday school class, feeling blessed that I had a few more years left on the planet than they did, since they were older.

The only person I knew even a little who'd died was Mr. Emily, who attended our church. Tragically, he drowned one day while gigging frogs. The church was full of sorrow over this for weeks, but I knew that young Mr. Emily was the exception. Death was as far away as the ice age that my teachers swore was approaching.

Most of all, I loved to read the church statistics printed in *The Messenger*. They say preachers are all about numbers, but I can't imagine Dr. Silver studying them with more passion than I did. I felt let down any Sunday we didn't bring in at least 450 soul, and I was rooting for over 800 each Easter. I tried subtracting one Sunday's attendance from another's in my head, and it's no wonder I became pretty good at math with all that practice.

After I'd mined all the gold I could out of *The Messenger,* I turned my attention to the little registration cards and envelopes in their wooden pew holders. These wooed me like candy, but Mom forbid me from writing on them. "The church had to pay good money for those! We're not going to be wasteful by scribbling all over them, now are we?" No, we were not. But I'll admit to coveting them a little bit, especially on Sundays when the sermon ran long.

The passing of the offering plate was always good for a little potential action as well. I'd reach toward it hesitantly, hopefully, as it made its way down the pew, but Dad usually intercepted the shiny plate before I could make contact. There was good reason for this, since anyone who'd attended First Baptist for more than a month could tell an unfortunate tale of a dropped offering plate. These events were loud, especially when they occurred in a row full of coin-favoring children.

If the passing of the offering plate was a privilege, it was nothing compared to the honor of passing of the communion plate. The tray with the wafers was not so tricky, but the shining silver plate full of little cups of grape juice was an accident waiting to happen. I knew that I wasn't allowed to take communion until I accepted Jesus as my Savior, but I wished I could at least touch that layered tray. It held as much mystery as the Ark of the Covenant, and each time it traveled down the row, the adults on either side of me passed it high above my grasp. I was reduced to following it with my eyes, watching the purple liquid bubble and sway inside each tiny cup.

Apparently, the age at which one was trusted to safely pass the plates was closely tied to the age of accountability, and I wasn't there yet.

Chapter 9 – Sweet, Sweet Spirit

There's a sweet sweet spirit in this place
And I know that it's the spirit of the Lord
There are sweet expressions on each face
And I know that it's the presence of the Lord

Sweet Holy Spirit,
Sweet Heavenly Dove,
Stay right here with us
Filling us with your love

And for these blessings
We lift our hearts in praise
Without a doubt we'll know that we have been revived
When we shall leave this place

"Let's pray," Dad said, as we bowed our heads over the hamburger stroganoff. And right then, the phone rang. Jill jumped up from the kitchen table, picked up the receiver, and chirped, "Come Lord Jesus, be our guest, and let thy gifts to us be blessed, amen!" Her eyes grew as big as saucers when she realized she'd just greeted the caller with our supper prayer.

This incident passed forever into the family archives when the caller turned out to be none other than Mrs. Silver, the preacher's wife. She was wondering if their son Stan could stay at our house for the weekend while she and Dr. Silver went out of town.

Stan was a teenager, and Jill and I preferred peeking shyly at him around corners to actually speaking with him. Still, we cleaned the house and tidied up for his visit just as we would have had Moses dropped in. Mom made steaks from cows Papaw had butchered and fixed her special cheesecake for dessert. The presence of guests always resulted in better eating than usual.

Since my mom was church pianist, the minister of music and his family were prime supper guest candidates. So when Reverend Shreve arrived as minister of music, Mom wasted no time in inviting him and his family over.

Reverend and Mrs. Shreve were fine, upstanding, godly people. Their daughter, Amy, became a minor celebrity at First Baptist because of her contention that "Bringing in the Sheaves" was actually titled "Bringing in the *Shreves*." A hymn was named after her family! This tale made its way into church conversations often, never failing to elicit smiles and gentle headshakes from the women telling it. *Bringing in the* ***Shreves****! So precious!*

But the Shreves' son Phillip was another story. Phillip was what could charitably be called ornery. He was a pill, a real pistol. When we sang about the joy, joy, joy, joy, down in our hearts, and how if the devil didn't like it he could sit on a tack, Phillip was the loudest one shouting "OUCH!" He quickly gained a reputation at church, and in our home as well.

The day after the Shreves' supper visit, my mom discovered that the can of Hershey's syrup in the fridge had chocolate running down the side and smeared on the opening. She was convinced that Phillip Shreve was the cause of this, and all our eyes grew wide as we pictured Phillip *actually drinking the Hershey's syrup! Right out of the can!* No additional evidence ever tied Phillip to this crime, but it lived on in family lore.

Over the years, other ministers of music visited our table as well. Hospitality was a high calling, and it always tended to make me a little jittery. I was so nervous that I spilled a glass of water all over Mr. Hatfield, who served as interim music director since he was still taking seminary classes. It took me years to live down my mortification.

***

"You girls can sit with Mrs. Gilbert tonight," Mom told Jill and me.

Hmmmm. My mind went to work at once, because this had possibilities. It was a rare occasion that my sister and I didn't sit with our parents in church. But on this particular Sunday night, Mom was playing piano and Dad was sitting behind the pulpit along with the pastor and minister of music, due to his deacon of the week status.

I was usually content with what I had, but sometimes I envied kids with lenient parents. Those kids frequently walked out during the middle of church services, only to reappear ten or fifteen minutes later.

I wondered what that would be like. I knew enough not to ask my dad if I could get up and leave in the middle of church, but Jill would ask sometimes. She was always met with a raised eyebrow and a firmly-mouthed "WAIT."

But ah, Mrs. Gilbert. She was a cheery lady with blonde hair and bright lipstick. She always sat in the dead-center of the sanctuary, near the front. I was pretty sure she wasn't German.

So, after Dr. Silver had been preaching for awhile, I nonchalantly pulled an offering envelope out of the pew ahead of me and began doodling on it, although this didn't feel nearly as fulfilling as I'd imagined. If Mrs.Gilbert noticed my wastefulness, she showed no sign. I had hit the jackpot.

There was just one frontier left to conquer, and I was feeling adventurous. I casually whispered to her, "Can I please go to the bathroom?"

She beamed at me. "Why, sure!" She turned her knees to the side so that I could slide out quickly, and I did.

What a feeling it was, walking down the aisle to the front of the church. Somehow, the same aisle I'd deliberated over walking to accept Christ seemed a whole lot less intimidating right now. I waltzed right out the side door, leaving the sanctuary and the service behind me.

I stood for just a moment in the strangely empty hallway, pondering my first move. The lights were dim and the only human in sight was an usher, pacing the far end of the corridor. I wandered over to the nursery and peeked in, waving to the smiling nursery workers and a few crying toddlers.

Although I didn't need to, I visited the bathroom next, since I wanted to keep my rationale for leaving honest. There I spent some quality time with my good friends, the disembodied children of the world stickers stuck on the back of the stall door.

A leisurely stop at the drinking fountain rounded out my break, and I retraced my steps back to my seat. I slid past Mrs. Gilbert, who was still smiling at me.

Dr. Silver was preaching full-bore, and he hadn't even yet said, "And so, my friends …", so I knew he still had a way to go.

I shivered happily in the pew, reliving my escapade. I knew it wouldn't be something I could hope to repeat, and I was trying my hardest not to make eye contact with either my mom or my dad, who I figured were quite ready to yank a knot in my tail. But I would remember it forever: my adventure out of the sanctuary. It was my version of Dorothy traveling through the Land of Oz.

Chapter 10 – Jesus Wants Me for a Sunbeam

Jesus wants me for a sunbeam, to shine for Him each day.
In every way try to please Him, at home, at school, at play.
A sunbeam, a sunbeam, Jesus wants me for a sunbeam!
A sunbeam, a sunbeam, I'll be a sunbeam for Him.

I loved choir, except for the singing part. Church choir was the place to be on Thursday afternoons after school for the children of First Baptist. We gathered in the choir room, a cheery place with tall windows along the back wall and metal chairs made more intriguing by the addition of little desktops that you could slide up and lock into place with your right hand.

The choir room was a place of many doors. One led to the minister of music's office, and another to the dark and somewhat creepy choir robe room, full of robes current and past. It was a favorite pastime of the church's youngest members to run back and forth under these robes, the hems brushing their hair, until their moms scolded them and reminded them that this was God's house, even the robe room.

There was another door leading to the church library, which doubled as the room where we ate refreshments after choir each week. I had spent many hours in the church library while Dad and Mom attended deacon and deaconess meetings, and it was cool beyond what you'd expect for a simple paneled room lined with bookshelves. One wall featured my favorite picture of Jesus. He stood at a door knocking, and I'd learned that this was the door to my heart. It was amazing to realize that the door to my heart was made of heavy boards and featured a nifty paned medieval peephole as well, surrounded by healthy vines. Jesus was positively glowing in a very God-like way. He looked so kind and so appealing that I couldn't imagine anyone not opening the door to sup with him.

And off of the library was the smallest kitchen I'd ever seen, tantalizingly dubbed The Kitchenette. It had just a fridge, a stove, and a sink, and was only big enough for maybe two ladies to pour the communion grape juice and line up the little wafers onto their silver trays. Choir moms filled the kitchenette each week, bringing in snickerdoodles and Kool-Aid and serving them to us with a smile.

Our choir played games and learned about hymn composers through little comics drawn by the minister of music, Reverend Shreve. Reverend Shreve's technique for grabbing our attention involved depicting each comic composer as a fruit. And it must have worked, because Sabine Baring-Gould, the composer of "Onward, Christian Soldiers" -- and also a grape -- fascinated me more than Wonder Woman ever did.

***

"It's Cool in the Furnace," our children's choir musical about Shadrach, Meshach, and Abednego, offered me the welcome chance to play the glockenspiel. I only had to play three different notes, over and over, which was ridiculously easy since I already took piano lessons and had a base threshold of intelligence.

On the night of the performance, I approached the instrument only to find that Reverend Shreve, apparently doubting my abilities, had removed each of the keys except the three I needed. I was a bit offended by what I felt sure was a vote of no confidence, but I donged out those three notes, over and over, with exuberance.

But I couldn't make it through the entire children's church music program just playing the glockenspiel, although I would have enjoyed trying. Eventually, I had to sing.

Mom thought it would be neat for Jill and me to minister to the congregation through singing, and so when Reverend Shreve passed around a sign-up sheet for special music on Sunday nights, she signed us up quicker than Saul lost his vision on the road to Damascus. We stumbled through "Jesus Wants Me for a Sunbeam," even more or less hitting the high note for *beam*, but I formed the firm opinion that solos and duets were not my spiritual gift.

Reverend Shreve was unaware of this, however, and I often ended up with a singing part in musicals, due in large part to my faithful attendance.

He was giving out spring musical parts one Thursday, and I was beginning to feel relieved because the vast majority had been assigned.

"Okay, one final song, 'Where Do We Go From Here?' Let's see. It's a full choir number up until the ending phrase ..."

Fingers crossed, fingers crossed ...

"And, I'd like to have Susan sing that to finish out the song. That'll wrap it up! Be sure to work on your lines and singing parts, and we'll start work next week. Okay, off for refreshments!"

Uh oh. I uncrossed my fingers, which was actually a bit difficult because they were now sweaty. I could feel the blood draining from my extremities. Not only did I have a solo, but my solo also finished up the whole musical! That meant that I would have to make it through the entire performance with that awful sense of foreboding, and I'd be the last thing everyone remembered. Additionally, the phrase ascended to a high D, which my alto voice struggled to even reach. I decided to make an appeal to Mom.

I hopped into the car, set my satchel next to me, and pulled no punches. "Mom, Reverend Shreve gave me a solo, but I don't want to do it! Do I have to?"

"Susan, being chosen for a solo is quite an honor! Now, why wouldn't you want to do it?"

I leaned back into the seat. What kind of answer could I give to that question? None that was very convincing, I was sure of that. I turned and looked out the window in silence, taking in the familiar sights with the longing a prisoner on death row must feel. Pizza Palace. Dairy Delight. Ah, to enjoy those simple pleasures without the spectre of a solo hanging over my head!

Mom remained silent, but I knew she was cooking up something. When we got home, she marched through the kitchen, straight to the bookshelf, and pulled out "Just a Box?" which was a recent purchase from the Scholastic Book order. I loved paging through the book orders my teacher sent home, and occasionally Mom would select a book she deemed "a good one." She would send the teacher a note with the money, informing her that this was a surprise. And thus, I became the recipient of "A Bargain for Frances," "Sad Day, Glad Day," and my personal favorite, "Dear Garbage Man." "Just a Box" had been our only foray into non-fiction. But it was a decidedly wonderful book. It showed illustrations for how to make almost anything from a box. A basket, a zoo (including cages with bars), an Indian village -- all things were possible, apparently, if you only had a box, glue, and some construction paper.

Holding the book in front of her, Mom gave it her best shot: "If you sing the solo, I'll help you make *anything you want* in this book."

Wow. "Anything?"

Mom flipped through the book for dramatic effect. "Anything."

In that moment, I saw my future, and it involved singing a solo. It also involved a very cool dollhouse, made from a box, which opened up and had two stories, a chimney, and furniture.

***

"Where Do We Go From Here?" was drawing to a close. I made my way down the risers toward the microphone, almost losing my footing as I squeezed between Dwayne and Betsy.

I stood before the microphone, quaking in my shoes and remembering to look above the heads of the congregation, who were regular people just like me who put their pants on one leg at a time, after all, and listened for my cue. *Dollhouse,* I thought, *dollhouse.*

Where do we go from here, precious Jesus? Where do we go from here?
Now that you've taken every sin away, now that you've come into my heart to stay.
Please tell me, where do we go from here, precious Jesus? Where do we go from here?

I leaned in to the microphone: *"Anywhere with you in control of my life will be alright with me."*

And just that fast, it was history. I turned and quickly climbed the risers again, with a blush and a ridiculously happy smile on my face. I'd been a sunbeam for Jesus **and** earned a dollhouse in the process.

Chapter 11 – Tell Me the Story of Jesus

Tell me the story of Jesus, write on my heart every word;
Tell me the story most precious, sweetest that ever was heard.
Tell how the angels in chorus sang as they welcomed His birth,
"Glory to God in the highest! Peace and good tidings to earth."

"What did Samson look like?" Laura asked. Usually she wasn't too interested in such things, but the prospect of a good-looking, long-haired rebel was a little more intriguing than another tale of Moses and the Children of Israel.

"Maybe Donny Osmond," Bekki said, a dreamy smile on her face.

"We don't really know," Miss Harrington replied, "other than that he had long hair."

I smiled, because I had a little secret: I did know what Samson looked like.

***

Each night after supper, Dad read us a story from the big Bible storybook. Even though the book was huge, we'd been through it cover to cover more than once, and you would have a hard time coming up with a Bible story I didn't know.

Sometimes, my illusions were shattered. Mom shared with me one day that Goliath, the mighty giant, was nine feet tall.

"That's about as tall as our patio is long," she said as she passed the mashed potatoes.

"That's all?" I was appalled, because I could cover the patio in three strides of my best attempt at skipping. In my mind, Goliath had always been at least 30 feet tall. He was a **giant**, for Pete's sake, not a candidate for the basketball team. My thrill over the David and Goliath story was forever diminished.

But we had more sources of Biblical knowledge. My Aunt Elaine, who was studying to be a missionary in Africa, had given Jill and me "The Bible in Pictures for Little Eyes." Since she was a prospective missionary, I knew that it had to be good, and it was. The book came with a stack of 45 RPM records, and Jill and I spent numerous rainy afternoons lying on the floor, listening to the narrator's deep, deep, James Earl Jones-like voice as he read story after story after story. We never moved, except to obey his command to TURN THE PAGE.

And what pages they were! Each one contained a story and a large picture. These weren't just any pictures, but lushly colorful, detailed windows into Bible times. They brought the entire Bible to life for me, and my mental images of many Biblical scenes forever after became those I'd viewed there. The tower of Babel would always look like an upside-down ice cream cone, leaning like the Tower of Pisa. Abraham, being told by God that his descendants would be like the stars of the sky, would always be pondering the vast darkness with one hand anchored on a rock, inclining in a Raphaelesque way toward the heavens.

Any thoughts I entertained about disobeying were soundly quashed when I viewed the picture of the naughty Children of Israel who disobeyed Moses, only to have the ground open up and swallow them. One man, desperately grasping at a tree root as he fell into the center of the earth, never failed to terrify me, and there are quite a few creases in the page to this day. I could stare for hours at the picture of Adam and Eve leaving the Garden of Eden, Eve sobbing as she leaned into Adam, who was looking back at the lush ferns wistfully. It was sorrow defined.

Another story to ponder was that of the Angel of Death passing over and killing all the Egyptian first-borns. I looked at the picture of the weeping Egyptian mother hovering over her son and read, "In this picture everyone is crying. Do you know why? It is because the king's oldest boy has died. God's angel came and the boy died because there was no blood on the door." Being the oldest girl, I wondered frequently whether I would have survived, had I been an ancient Egyptian. Did first-born daughters face slaughter as well, or was this one of the few perks to being female in the BC era? These were the kinds of questions I had, but neither sermons nor Sunday school classes ever seemed to get around to them.

The stories accompanying the pictures were short, but powerful. There was no candy-coating for kids in this book, no siree bob. "God gave Abraham a little baby boy just as he promised" is followed fast by "Soon Abraham will take out his knife to kill his dear son." Another tale starts out, "Why is this man lying here so still? It is because he is dead." But as harsh as these simple tales often were, I couldn't tear myself away from them. It was like National Geographic for the church set: cruel, but all a part of God's big story.

The man lying down on the floor is dead. The man standing up is Peter. Peter was sitting there and the man came in and told him a lie. As soon as he told the lie he suddenly fell down and died. God punished Ananias because he told a lie. Soon the people will carry him outside and make a hole and put him in it and cover him up.

Such stories took the thrill out of fibbing about whether I'd eaten the last cookie in the cookie jar, that was for sure.

Not every story in the book was scary; some were downright familiar and comforting. I learned that Jesus must indeed have been Baptist, because the story of his first miracle informed me that the folks at the wedding at Cana "needed more grape juice to drink." It was sure a relief to know that Jesus hadn't been drinking wine. And when Hannah prayed that God would give her a baby, she was at "church" and the "minister" saw her! I could just picture her down at the First Baptist altar, with Dr. Silver peeking in at the side door.

***

When I could contain myself no longer, I raised my hand.

"Miss Harrington, I do know what Samson looked like. He did have long brown hair, and it was wavy. It went about to his shoulders. He also wore those Bible-timey sandals, and he wore a purple robe. Except when he pulled down the building at the end of the story, and then he wore a loincloth and a red robe."

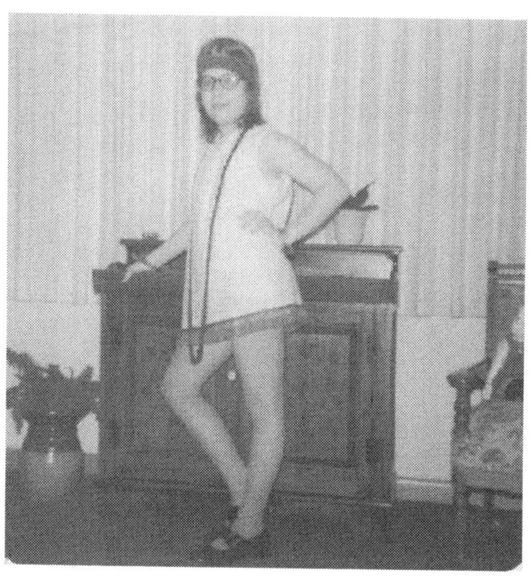

Chapter 12 – Oh, Be Careful Little Eyes

Oh, be careful little eyes, what you see.
Oh, be careful little eyes, what you see.
For the Father up above is looking down in love,
So be careful little eyes, what you see.

Oh, be careful little ears what you hear…
Be careful little mouth what you say...
Be careful little hands, what you touch...
Be careful little feet, where you go...

I gazed longingly at the girls on the stage. Although they were my age, we were worlds apart. These girls wore colorful lycra costumes, complete with sequins and jewels. Music blared from loudspeakers set up on the outdoor platform, and the girls began to dance. There were always one or two who had more talent than the others, and my eyes were drawn to them. It was just another performance by kids from Dixon's Dance Studio at the local Seymour Oktoberfest. The whole production was decidedly low-rent, but it seemed like Broadway to me. I wondered what it would feel like to be up there, dancing on stage.

In line at recess, I would arrange my feet into fifth position and rise up to a tentative releve. "Are you in ballet?" the recess teacher asked.

"No," I wistfully replied. Because, while dancing wasn't an out-and-out *sin*, it also wasn't purely wholesome. And I really and truly wished it was. Each week when Mom and Jill and I watched *The Lawrence Welk Show*, the dancers Bobby and Cissy were by far my favorite act.

I grew up knowing that some activities were righteous, others questionable, and some downright sinful. As Baptists, our definition of sin was broader than that of some others.

Mom taught me from an early age: "Susan, when you get older, people will try to get you to smoke or drink. You know, you just have to say no!"

I swallowed this admonition hook, line, and sinker, and for years, each time a new student moved in, I'd eye her curiously. Was this the one who would attempt to defraud me of my virtuous character by offering me a cigarette or a can of beer? The irony didn't escape me that the peers most likely to lead me astray were the kids I knew from church.

I was 100% sure smoking was a sin. Sure, it wasn't specifically mentioned in the Bible, but you know that verse about your body being the Lord's temple? You wouldn't pollute the Lord's temple with a cigarette, now would you? Same went for drinking, although that was a bit more problematic. After all, the Lutherans and Catholics in town were okay with drinking (our parents cautioned us *not* to drink from the sparkling fountain at Catholic wedding receptions). And there was that troublesome verse where Paul told Timothy to drink a little wine for his stomach. What could he have been thinking, although it was usually explained that Paul gave Timothy this concession because the water quality in Bible times was so suspect that wine was more acceptable back then.

Since most of our friends were Baptist as well, I had never witnessed a drunk person. At least, I didn't think so. When Mr. Sutton, our Lutheran neighbor, walked me home from babysitting his kids one night and paused at the end of the driveway to shake hands with one of our sunflowers before beginning a conversation with it, I figured he was just showing early signs of dementia. He did seem pretty young for that, though.

We visited a Lutheran church one Sunday, and while perusing the hymnal, I was shocked to discover a verse of "Let Us Break Bread Together" reading *Let us drink wine together on our knees.* I poked Jill and pointed to this subversive lyric, and we stared at each other in wide-eyed horror. It was scandalous to imagine drinking wine together on my knees with anyone, but in church, no less! I knew that the real words to that verse went, *Let us drink the cup together on our knees.* And what was in the cup? Grape juice, of course.

I was firm in my convictions that drinking, smoking, tattoos, piercings, and anything else questionable was out of the question for me, and I worried about others who did these things. "He's going to get cancer!" mom recorded me saying at age six of Santa Claus -- you know, that little round pipe he held tight in his teeth, and the smoke it encircled his head like a wreath -- I was sure that this would end in nothing good for jolly old Saint Nick.

Even the TV held some dangers. *I Dream of Jeannie* featured a genie, which was kind of like witchcraft, I supposed, and she wore a skimpy, inappropriate costume to make it even worse. And *Bewitched* was suspect as well, with its admittedly tame-looking witch. I knew that whenever *I Dream of Jeannie* or *Bewitched* appeared on the screen, I had best keep on changing the channel.

Chaste as my moral upbringing was, it was still much looser than Mom's had been. She told stories about her deeply conservative Christian childhood, and how her parents had forbidden movies, television, playing cards, and even nail polish. Mom solemnly recounted her memories of sitting at the supper table and trying to eat without her parents noticing the polish she had so scandalously applied.

I considered this as I did a series of quick twirls in my bedroom, trying to spot with my head so that I wouldn't get dizzy, and remembering to keep my feet turned out. I thought ballet still might be a little holy. It involved the color pink, and how could that be bad?

***

I held out the remote control, flipping through the TV channels. *The Love Boat* -- boring. *Bewitched* -- sinful. A movie with a soaring musical background -- boring.

I was babysitting at Suttons'. The kids had been asleep for hours, and at one in the morning I was dangerously close to dozing off myself. I wandered into the kitchen and opened up the fridge. Fruit, yogurt, pop … hmmmm … a half-full bottle of wine nestled in the back corner.

Curiosity got the better of me as I pulled it out and turned the bottle around. The liquid inside didn't look so threatening. It appeared kind of like Coke with a reddish hue. Slowly, slowly I loosened the cork, all the time visualizing myself dumping the whole thing across the kitchen carpet. But the cork finally eased out and I took a sniff. It smelled a little like something had died in there.

Opening the cabinet, I took out a Fred Flintstone cup, shocked at my own actions. I poured a half-inch of wine into the glass and swirled the liquid around and around. Should I taste it? I knew it was sinful, but somehow I didn't feel like God would punish me for one taste of wine when others had taken so many more.

I raised the cup to my lips, but then another thought occurred to me. The health teacher had talked about alcohol, just last week, and she'd told us how alcohol reached the brain two minutes after being drank. It killed brain cells, and those cells would never come back.

I eyed the foul-smelling liquid with an awful mix of curiosity and disgust. Some of my school classes were pretty hard, and I didn't know that I could afford to lose a lot of brain cells. Then again, it was only a half-inch worth of liquid.

Oh, whatever! I tipped back my head and drank, not the whole half-inch, but just a tiny sip, to play it extra safe. And it tasted -- like nail polish remover! Or a really awful kind of medicine! Quickly, and with a feeling of utter relief, I poured the remaining liquid down the drain, shoved the cork back into the bottle and returned it to its spot in the fridge. All the while, I offered up a fervent prayer that Mr. and Mrs. Sutton wouldn't choose that moment to arrive back home and find their teenage babysitter drinking wine in the kitchen.

I poured myself a glass of grape juice, which tasted mercifully like communion, to get that awful taste out of my mouth.

I headed back to the living room, switched to the *Love Boat,* and watched it with a new, more worldly perspective. For I had drunk of the fruit of the vine, and although I knew I had sinned a little in so doing, I had proved to myself that the devil liquor would never be a snare to me. I couldn't stand the taste, and this knowledge was surely worth losing a few brain cells.

Chapter 13 – Lo, How a Rose E'er Blooming

Lo, how a Rose e'er blooming from tender stem hath sprung,
of Jesse's lineage coming, as men of old have sung.
It came, a flow'ret bright, amid the cold of winter,
when half-spent was the night.

When I grew up, I wanted to be a Mouseketeer. I knew that the odds of this actually happening were slim, but I figured my chances were at least as good as Todd's to get into the NFL, or Kim's to be Miss America.

Jill and I loved to watch The Mickey Mouse Club on TV. We grew up with reruns of Annette and Darlene. But our enthusiasm (or perhaps I should say *my* enthusiasm, because, although Jill was a good follower, I was generally the one calling the shots at home) knew no limits when The New Mickey Mouse Club began. The boy Mouseketeers didn't do a lot for me, but the girls! Ah, I was taken with them every one, from impressive Lisa and pony-tailed Julie to Kelly with the Farrah Fawcett hair and impossibly cute little Mindy. The bright neon-hued jumpsuits, the colorful sets, the singing, the dancing -- what a dream it would be to join them on TV.

Because, while I was terribly awkward when it came to singing in church, I had no doubt that I would be totally transformed on the Disney stage. I'd belt out "The Who What Why Where When and How Day" with the best of them! I'd dance up a storm, and I had a pretty good feeling that, since it was The Mickey Mouse Club, this kind of dancing didn't count as sinful.

In my excitement, I persuaded Jill, Miriam, and countless others to spend hours copying Mouseketeer routines. We could perform the "Surprise Day, Surprise Day, Let's Open Up Our Eyes Day" opening with a flair to rival that of any of the real Mouseketeers. The playhouse porch formed an excellent stage, and we perfected our acts over and over again.

***

My chances for fame as a Mouseketeer may have been slim and fading fast, but I did have the chance to be a rosebud. Every Wednesday night.

First Baptist had a Wednesday night class for elementary girls, dubbed Rosebuds by its founder, Aunt Phyllis. Phyllis wasn't our aunt, but that didn't stop any of us from calling her that anyway. Aunt Phyllis was generous, both in size and in spirit, and had what Mom called "personality plus!"

Aunt Phyllis was a bit of a character. She wasn't an old lady, but neither was she young. Her black permed hair, along with her fondness for bright colors and loud floral prints, made her easy to spot as she traveled the halls of First Baptist. She often accessorized her dresses with pillbox hats, and her horn-rimmed glasses did nothing to dim her sparkling eyes. When she finally married several years later, I was not a bit surprised to see her walk down the aisle in a pink tinted gown.

Grandma Short, her mother, was Aunt Phyllis's constant companion. Viewed together, they brought to mind David and Goliath, with Grandma Short being as petite as Aunt Phyllis was big and tall. Grandma Short was into crafts of all types. Her Christmas tree ornaments crafted from brightly painted light bulbs were famous throughout the congregation.

I don't know if Aunt Phyllis had a job or any other pastime at all outside of her activities at First Baptist, but in my mind, her sole occupation was teaching Rosebuds. She had seemingly led the group forever, and her goal of nurturing us young rosebuds seemed as iffy a proposition as me becoming a Mouseketeer.

"You girls are just like beautiful rosebuds!" she'd tell us so sincerely, over and over. Rhoda giggled at this, and Laura and I eyed each other skeptically.

"You haven't blossomed yet, but you will! And then, you will be roses in full bloom, making the world so beautiful!"

I'm not sure what it was, but when Aunt Phyllis said it, I could almost believe it. Whether it was her appearance, her enthusiasm, or the sheer force of her personality, everyone behaved in her class. Nobody talked sassy or ignored another girl. She expected us to be young ladies, she led by example, and somehow it worked, at least a little bit.

Aunt Phyllis liked to give her rosebuds little booklets on special occasions, such as the end of another Rosebud year. Many of these had titles like *Bits of Silver and Gold for Girls,* and they were filled with gauzy photos of flowers and sayings like *To have a friend, be a friend.*

But my favorite Aunt Phyllis booklet was tiny, entitled *Bible Messages for Every Day.* It contained a list of months, with a short Bible verse for each day.

I knew that it was dangerous to just pop open the Bible randomly, hoping for guidance. After all, I'd heard the familiar church joke about the man who, in a fit of depression, flipped open his Bible to Matthew 27:5: *And Judas went … and hanged himself.* Feeling even worse, the poor guy then flipped to Luke 10:37: *Go thou and do likewise.*

But I figured that it was A-okay to read the daily verse, and I marveled at that little book, because each day when I'd read the verse, it was just what I needed to hear. How could it be that I would face a bully on June 1, when the verse was *Fret not thyself because of evildoers*? Or that I'd need to muster a bit more faith on November 11, when I read *Whoso trusteth in the Lord, happy is he*? I viewed the booklet as one of life's small miracles, because God spoke to me through it time after time.

***

August 16, 1977, Elvis died. I learned this at Rosebuds, where Laura met me in the hallway.

"Did you know Elvis died?"

Indeed, I did not. My dad was an Elvis fan, but other than occasionally hearing "Jailhouse Rock" on the 8-track tape, I was pretty clueless about the King.

"Well, he did. He was doing drugs. His little girl, Lisa Marie, is only nine."

I stopped for a moment, absorbing this. Here was a great real-life example of the evils of drug use. Why couldn't Elvis have just said no when someone handed him that marijuana? While I wouldn't miss him much, I felt a wave of sorrow for the now-fatherless Lisa Marie. She and I were almost the same age, and yet I doubted that she would have the chance to become a rosebud. Without Elvis around, could she bloom?

Laura and I headed solemnly into class, contemplating the brevity of life. We did a few Bible sword drills, heard a brief lesson on how to act like young ladies, and made tray favors out of communion cups, little plastic flowers, and glue for folks in the nursing home. We made tray favors often enough that we had surely blessed every senior citizen in the state with them twice or more. At least, it seemed that way.

And then, having come one week closer to blooming, we stood in a circle and clasped hands for the Rosebud closing ritual.

"May the Lord watch between me and thee, while we are absent, one from another," we recited, and none of us was even tempted to laugh, chew gum, or give each other bunny ears.

I looked up at Aunt Phyllis and she winked at me. It seemed like anything was possible, whether that involved becoming a Mouseketeer or simply blooming.

Chapter 14 – Climb, Climb Up Sunshine Mountain

Climb, climb up sunshine mountain
Heavenly breezes blow
Climb, climb up sunshine mountain
Faces all aglow
Turn, turn from sin and sorrow
Look to God on high
Climb, climb up sunshine mountain
You and I

Only two things were certain in summertime: 4-H and Vacation Bible School. I spent the first weeks of summer committed to 4-H projects, as I attempted to sew straight seams, iron them open, and clip all my threads. Then I whipped up batch after batch of cookies, leveling each cup of flour off with a knife to make it perfect, and counting to ensure each cookie had the same number of chocolate chips, because if it were close between me and another girl to see who would be champion, the judge just might do that.

The county fair, held in late July, was one of the year's highlights. But when 4-H and the fair ended, there was no time to feel let down, because their pleasant insanity was replaced with that of a different kind, in the form of Vacation Bible School.

Vacation Bible School, or VBS as we insiders knew it, was quite an undertaking. In those days when almost every family had a mom at home all day, the volunteers were plentiful and thus the program was ambitious. VBS ran for two weeks, for three hours each weekday morning.

Housewives whose talents were underutilized for most of the year had their chance to shine during VBS as they traded in their aprons for Sonshine Mountain nametags.

The first morning of VBS dawned sunny and hot. Mom hustled Jill and me through a quick breakfast of Pop Tarts, and into the car. Then it was off to church -- in shorts. VBS was the one occasion when it was deemed acceptable to wear pants, or even, heaven forbid, shorts, to God's house. Jill and I took full advantage, because it was a little tricky doing the crab walk in a skirt. Still, walking into church with fabric between our legs felt a little scandalous.

Mom dropped us off at the church's front lawn, which was covered by approximately 5,000 kids and adults. At least, that was my estimate. The kids milled around, looking for an adult holding up a large sign with "Primary 1" or "4's and 5's" written in fat magic marker. Just when the lawn appeared to reach its capacity, the church bus pulled in.

First Baptist had a full-size church bus, actually an old, repainted school bus. Volunteers for the Bus Ministry drove into the bad part of town (which didn't differ much from the good part in Seymour) to pick up unchurched kids who were willing to come try VBS for the morning. Dozens of moms in the bad part of town breathed a sigh of relief for three hours of freedom, and dozens more kids poured out of the bus as it opened its rickety door.

Jill had found her leader and gotten into line, but I was still looking. I wished fervently for a good lead teacher, because the lead teacher could make or break VBS. Okay, there she was -- Mrs. Westfall. I didn't know much about her, but she looked perky. I said a little prayer for God to grant her competence, and got into line next to Bekki.

"Look!" she said, shoving a dog-eared paperback at me. "I just finished this book. It is so good. You have to read it! Promise!"

I turned over the book. It was called "Devil in a Dark Blue Suit," and while the man on the cover didn't look like my idea of the devil, he didn't look entirely wholesome either.

"I'm kind of busy with reading now. I have a list of books I need to read for the library summer reading club."

Bekki hit me over the head jokingly with the book. "Aw, you're no fun! Always reading Nancy Drew or something like that! I'll get you to read this someday. Here we go!"

We paraded into the sanctuary behind our leader, walking until we reached the pew marked with our class name. This was not the sanctuary I knew from Sunday morning. It had been given new life as Sonshine Mountain, and I stared appreciatively at all the trees made from carpet roll tubes and acres of crepe paper. The altar table up front was gone, replaced by giant papier mache rocks. An urgent call for stuffed animals in last week's *Messenger* had apparently been successful, because they filled the podium area with an abundance not seen since Noah's Ark.

"Awright!" the VBS song leader shouted from the podium. Volume and enthusiasm were the two requirements for song leader, and she had both in spades.

"Welcome to Sonshine Mountain! We're gonna start out with 'Deep and Wide,' so make sure you're an arm's length from your neighbor, okay?"

The sanctuary was full of kids reaching out on each side of them, smacking others left and right. There was no way we could stand an arm's length from anyone in there, but we knew we had to try. Bible School songs, after all, were about nothing if not the hand motions.

Deep and wide,
Deep and wide,
There's a fountain flowing deep and wide
Deep and wide,
Deep and wide,

There's a fountain flowing deep and wide

"Great! Well, I'm just so glad you're all here with me today on Sonshine Mountain! Aren't you? We're gonna have so much fun! Aren't we?"

This was met with an anemic response, since many of the kids weren't even paying attention to her.

"C'mon, you can do better than that ... **aren't we?"**

The response this time was just marginally better.

"Okay, you guys forced me into it. Boys: aren't we gonna have fun?"

This approach never failed to produce an ear-splitting roar. "YES!"

"Okay, girls. You're not gonna let them win, are you? Girls, aren't we gonna have fun?"

"YES!"

"Wow, that's pretty close! I'll have to call it a tie! Hmmm … who's that I see sneaking around over there? Why, it's a big giant! I bet it's Goliath!"

I craned my neck around until I spied Rhoda's teenage brother at the edge of Sonshine Mountain, wearing a bathrobe and holding a stick. He had a bandana tied around his forehead.

"Now every time I say 'Goliath,' I want you guys to yell BOO! as loud as you can. Okay? Let's try it. 'GOLIATH.'"

"BOO!"

"Great! Okay, now who's this on the other side of the mountain?"

An unknown boy from the junior department, also sporting a bathrobe, peeked his head over the fake rocks.

"Jesus?" a little kid yelled out, and everyone laughed.

"Ha, well, that's a real good guess, honey, but I think we're a few thousand years before Jesus," the song leader shouted. "Any other ideas?"

"David!"

"You guys are so smart! Yes! It's David! See, he has a little pouch he's carrying. I wonder what could be in there?"

And so it went, until half the kids were hoarse from the thrill and novelty of making loud noises in the sanctuary, and the other half had to go to the bathroom, and then it was time for the offering.

Bible school offering was a big deal, and I was inspired by the big offering project each year. Dropping coins into the plate to help build a Sub-Saharan church had infinitely more appeal than shoving a dollar bill into the Sunday school offering basket for who-knew-what-purpose.

"This year, guys, we're collecting money to build a Christian school for kids in Guatemala," the song leader shared. A slide showing a tropical setting with a group of kids, naked as jaybirds, was flashed onto the screen behind her.

A wave of compassion swept over me, as I pictured a mass of poor kids sitting in a schoolroom, probably with a dirt floor, huddled around a single book. I knew that the first thing I'd do when I got home was to grab a screwdriver out of the junk drawer in the kitchen and use it to pry the stopper out of my Tony the Tiger bank. I'd count the change, dime by dime and penny by penny, and I'd put it into a little sack to bring the next day. I pondered ways I could bring in a little more by doing some extra chores at home. I was sure that the only thing standing between a Guatemalan orphan and a successful future might be the fifty cents I could earn if I only put my mind to it.

The offering plate made its slow trek down each row. I knew I could count on the tinkling clatter of change on the floor as the 4's and 5's class spilled their plate at least once, and each third grade boy worth his salt had to give the plate a loud shake as it passed. Once the tithes were all in the storehouse, the song leader dismissed us to our classrooms.

***

It was no secret that the number of kids who decided to accept Christ in any Bible school class was directly proportional to the storyteller's skill level. At one end of the spectrum were the teachers who read the story out of the book, and those were the teachers I didn't want to get.

On the other end was Mrs. Westfall. The Holy Spirit must have really anointed her, because not only did she have the entire story memorized each day, but she also acted out all the characters herself, complete with voices. She was Jesus and all 12 disciples. She was Paul. She was Mary. She was amazing.

At the end of the lesson, she directed us all to close our eyes, and said that if we'd decided to follow Jesus as our Savior, we should repeat this little prayer with her, in our hearts.

"Now, while everyone still has their eyes closed," she continued, "if you asked Jesus into your heart today, just slip up your hand right now. Nobody is going to see you …."

I confess, I had to open one eye just a crack. Sure enough, Kelly Hubbard and some boy I didn't know had their hands raised up to eye level. Mrs. Westfall cracked a huge grin and pumped her fist before saying, "Amen."

***

My favorite part of VBS was craft time. Crafts came naturally to me; I could knit and crochet, and I bet I could latch hook with my eyes closed. So I was practically salivating when Mrs. Westfall dropped a generous supply of yarn and Popsicle sticks onto the center of the table, and for the next 20 minutes my whole life revolved around creating an Eye of God. I wrapped and turned happily, repeating the Bible memory verse in my head and feeling about as happy as John on the island of Patmos when God gave him the revelation. When the diluted Kool-Aid and generic oreos came out, my contentment was complete.

"Kids, let's wrap things up here and do some sword drills," Mrs. Westfall called, amidst a flurry of tangled yarn.

I made a beeline for my Bible, because sword drills were another talent of mine. Sure, anyone could find John 3:16 or Genesis 1:1, but I could even find an obscure verse in Obadiah quicker than you could say "Can I get an amen?"

I loved to hear "Attention! Draw swords! Acts 12:5 … Charge!" We were off.

***

"Where are you girls at? Let's get this show on the road!" Mom blotted her lipstick on a square of toilet paper, which she left hanging on the roll because to throw it away would be wasteful.

"We can't be late for the closing program! Into the car, everyone!" Dad hollered, pulling up the garage door.

The Bible school closing program was always a great night at First Baptist, with a huge attendance resulting from all the parents of the VBS kids showing up at church.

Each class paraded into the sanctuary one last time, following our leaders with the big signs denoting our age. It was a noisy procession, although sometimes the teachers, with all their shushing, were just as loud as the kids.

Three sturdy children entered at the front, bearing the American flag, the Christian flag, and the Goliath-sized Bible. We began the service with a hearty pledge to the U.S. flag, followed by more feeble versions of the pledges to the Christian flag and the Bible, because hardly anyone knew the words to those.

The VBS song leader took her place at the podium for a final night.

"Welcome to Sonshine Mountain! We've had such a great time these last two weeks, and we'd like to show all you parents some of the things we've learned. How about 'Father Abraham,' guys?"

The energy level rose as we sang-shouted the tale of Father Abraham and his many sons, marching, turning, and sticking out our tongues as we made our undoubtedly joyful noises.

"Super! Now, it's time to announce the offering total. You know our goal was $500. Do you think we made it?"

"YES!" came the deafening roar.

"I'm not sure. Look at our chart here." The song leader moseyed over to the giant thermometer chart nestled in the rocks of Sonshine Mountain. "We only had $425 last time I checked. Let's see how much we took in on Friday ..."

I was so excited to hear the total that I could hardly stay in my seat. If we didn't raise $500, I didn't think I could stand it. Those kids in Guatemala were counting on us!

"You guys are not gonna believe this. I'm not sure I believe it!" The song leader looked truly surprised, or else she was a really good actor.

"We brought in 75 dollars and 32 cents. We made our goal! God is good! You guys are great!"

The sanctuary erupted in applause, and I don't think I'd ever clapped so hard, especially not in church.

The song leader challenged the parents to match the $500 we'd raised during that night's offering, and as I heard wallets opening all over the sanctuary, I knew they'd rise to the occasion. One thousand dollars for the Guatemalan school! My joy knew no bounds.

The organ played "Pass it On" as we ended the program with a slideshow of the week's events. We all pointed and laughed when we popped up in a slide, and hooted and hollered when a particularly embarrassing moment appeared for all the congregation to see.

Dr. Silver ended the program with an attempt at some dignity.

"Let's have a final prayer, and then we'd like to invite you all down to the Fellowship Center for a time of refreshment before leaving tonight."

Our family joined the throng walking the long hallway down to Fellowship Center, with Mrs. Westfall and her family beside us.

"Susan sure has enjoyed having you as a teacher," Mom confided in Mrs. Westfall, causing me to slink behind her in embarrassed silence.

"Oh, the pleasure's been all mine! She's a great girl," Mrs. Westfall said, grinning. "It has been so busy, though. We've had over 20 kids in class most days, and by the time I prepare the story and get the craft ready ..."

"Well, you know what they say. No rest for the wicked!" Mom said triumphantly, nodding and smiling in a jolly way.

I tugged at her sleeve. "Mom!" I whispered urgently. Mom was full of expressions, and sometimes they didn't come out quite right. I remembered last Christmas, when she'd opened a gift from a relative with the comment, "Well, you know what they say. It's the thought that counts, right?" I wanted to sink into the floor.

"Or something like that, at least!" Mom continued with a laugh, and Mrs. Westfall laughed right along. On the night of the VBS program, everything was construed in the best possible light.

Once we reached Fellowship Hall, Jill and I inched along the refreshment line, reaching for our melting scoops of ice cream in styrofoam bowls. The church hostesses stood sentinel on the other side of the table, faded floral aprons tied at their waists. One smiled at me, while another clucked her tongue and urged, "Easy now, easy!" to a couple of rowdy boys who were a little too eager with the Reddi-wip and the squirty bottles of chocolate syrup.

We fellowshipped for awhile with the others, both the regulars and the unchurched, who we fervently hoped might give First Baptist another try now that VBS had ended. And after the others had dwindled out, Jill and I ran around Fellowship Center (the one room in the church in which running was allowed), folding up the chairs and stacking them onto rolling racks.

"I thought the 'Climb This Mountain' song that everybody sang at the end was real pretty," Mom said as we walked lazily across the parking lot, the humidity as thick as those locusts back in Egypt.

"And that communion cup ornament you made was just super," Dad said to Jill, who was skipping along. "If it's okay, maybe I could take it to school to put on my desk?" Jill smiled happily and nodded.

Crickets chirped, mosquitoes buzzed, and our time at Sonshine Mountain had ended for another year.

Chapter 15 – Passed Through the Waters

Like survivors of the flood, like walkers through the sea,
like walkers through the God-divided sea,
We are rescued, we are claimed, we are loved and we are named;
We are baptized, I am baptized!
We have passed through the waters, and that's all that matters;
We have passed through the waters: O, thanks be to God!

Accepting Jesus as Savior was the first and greatest commandment, and the second was like unto it, Thou Shalt Be Baptized. I had no sooner recovered from walking the aisle to become a Christian than it struck me that I would need to be baptized. In the water.

I had never been what you'd call an active child, not by a long shot. My introspective nature led me to spend hours lying on my bed, reading books. I always kept a dictionary next to me so that I could look up any unfamiliar words. And while this endeared me to my teachers and led to good grades in school, it didn't do me any favors in the athletic department.

Mom signed Jill and me up for swimming lessons at the city pool so that we could conquer the water and achieve, as we did in other facets of life. But each summer morning as I donned my swimming suit, I was hit with a wave of nausea. If water were a person, I strongly suspected that he and I would not be friends. We probably wouldn't even be acquaintances.

My teenage instructor directed our class of five to dive underwater and retrieve pennies that she cavalierly tossed into the pool. I watched each one drop down, down, down, farther and farther away from me.

Is she kidding? I wondered. After all, wouldn't that require me to, first, keep myself underwater, and second, open my eyes in order to see the penny? There was no way that was going to happen, and even if it could, my near-sightedness made success extremely unlikely.

But she was serious, so I jumped in and madly searched for a penny with my toes. I hoped I could pick it up that way and somehow transfer it to my fingers without her noticing.

Considering my tenuous relationship with water, First Baptist's baptism by immersion scared me. Many nights as I'd watch Dr. Silver baptize new members, I'd feel a little twinge of regret that I wasn't Catholic or Lutheran. They got off awfully easy, I thought, since number one, they didn't have to walk down the aisle to become a Christian, and number two, their baptism involved the preacher dribbling a few drops of water onto their foreheads when they were babies. Who wouldn't be okay with that?

As a good Baptist, I would need to go the whole nine yards and be actually immersed -- *buried with Christ.* I wouldn't need to find a penny, true, but I would have to be dunked all the way under water. In front of a whole bunch of people.

Baptism was shrouded in mystery to me. I was intensely curious about the baptismal pool itself, which was in the front of the sanctuary, right behind the choir loft. I wasn't sure how deep it was, although Dr. Silver always seemed to be immersed up to his waist.

Even the baptismal waters enticed me, and I wondered whether they possessed magical qualities. After all, when Dr. Silver baptized someone, he wore a white robe under which I could plainly see a dress shirt and tie. However, he always returned to the sanctuary, fully clothed and dry, approximately two minutes after finishing baptisms. How could he get dry so quickly? How did his clothes stay dry? This mystified me, and my speculations usually put an end to any chance I'd had of paying attention to the evening's sermon.

Being buried with Christ in baptism didn't always go off without a hitch. Little kids sometimes struggled to keep their chins above the water, and this concerned me. I'd also witnessed more than one baptismal blooper, usually involving baptism candidates who were of the large variety. When one of these tall or portly folks descended into the pool, I sent up a little prayer that Dr. Silver would be able to pull him back up. After all, "body builder" wasn't a pastoral requirement, and I knew it couldn't be easy to pull a rather large, soaking-wet adult up out of the water.

I began praying fervently one night as a beefy man entered the baptismal waters. He gripped Dr. Silver's arm, check; went under, check; but then his feet slipped. This created a tidal wave, which splashed over the pool wall and into the choir loft, ruining the hairdos of the entire back row of the New Life Singers.

I spent many hours debating with myself whether baptism was truly necessary. After all, I'd learned in Sunday school that baptism didn't save a person. Salvation came only through accepting Jesus' death as payment for my sins. Still, baptism was a step of obedience, and I wouldn't be starting out my Christian walk too well by disobeying on a biggie like that.

***

Mom and I sat in the car in McDonald's parking lot while Dad and Jill ran in to get supper, our traditional and much-anticipated Sunday night treat. Dad bought a hamburger for each of us and a pack of fries to share, and we took it all home, so we wouldn't have to buy drinks at the restaurant. Tonight, however, I was going to be baptized, and this was impacting my appetite in a decidedly negative way.

"Susan, the decision you made to become a Christian is such a big deal. I don't even know how to explain it, really. It's probably the most important decision you'll ever make, other than maybe who to marry."

I squirmed in my seat, feeling a little awkward, as I always did when Mom broached a serious topic in a confined space like this. The comparison of walking down the aisle toward a future in heaven and walking down the aisle to get married struck me as odd. One involved a pretty dress and rainbow sherbet punch, but the other involved all eternity.

I wasn't sure how to put this thought into words, so I just said, "I'm not really that hungry. I don't think I want my Filet-O-Fish tonight."

"Oh, you'll want it later," Mom assured me. "I'll just heat it up in the double broiler when we get home from church. You'll be plenty hungry by then."

***

A smiling deaconess met me at the church doors that evening. She led me up the stairs into the labyrinth of rooms behind the sanctuary. Normally, the never-ending hallways with the mysterious doors opening off of them would have intrigued me, but tonight my teeth chattered and I was focused on one thing only: surviving baptism.

She opened the door to one of these rooms, which contained a rack full of white robes. Two other women, baptismal candidates as well, had arrived ahead of me, and they were already donned in robes. They looked sort of like angels, without the halo or wings.

"Let's see if we can find a small one -- here you go, this should work," Deaconess Lady said to me, holding a robe up to my shoulders and nodding. "Just put this on, and then we'll go find Dr. Silver."

I think I can, I think I can, I told myself, as I zipped the robe up.

"Well, hello, everyone!" Dr. Silver said, as we met him in yet another small, empty room. He was wearing his suit and carrying his Bible. "I'm so pleased that you're all taking the step of following

Christ in obedience through the act of baptism tonight. I'll show you what we'll do."

He demonstrated how we would enter the pool, grip his arm, lean back, and then finally (gloriously!) he would pull us up, to begin our new lives in Christ. I practiced, and was hugely gratified to note that he seemed to have no trouble pulling me up. *But,* I cautioned myself, *I know I'll be heavier in the water ...*

***

The service opened with baptism, and since I was a child, I was up first. I closed my eyes, took a deep breath, and descended the three steps into the pale green water -- thankfully, my chin cleared the top. I put a death grip on Dr. Silver's arm, as instructed, and time seemed to stand still as he placed a handkerchief over my nose, and dipped me down ... one second, two ... and raised me up, to newness of life.

I had survived! I was baptized, not only a child of God, but an obedient one as well!

Dr. Silver handed me off to the deaconess waiting at the steps on the other end of the pool, as he said, "I am the door, by me if any man enter, he shall be saved..."

I shivered like a wet dog, changed quickly back into my clothes, and happily returned to the sanctuary to take communion that night for the first time. The little wafer and cup of grape juice were no longer forbidden to me.

Back at home, I discovered that Mom had been right. When I ate my warmed-up Filet-O-Fish, as a new creation, it had never tasted so good.

Chapter 16 – In My Heart There Rings a Melody

I have a song that Jesus gave me
It was sent from heaven above;
There never was a sweeter melody
'Tis a melody of love.

In my heart there rings a melody
There rings a melody with heaven's harmony;
In my heart there rings a melody
There rings a melody of love!

Even Dr. Silver needed a break sometimes. Preaching every Sunday morning, Sunday night, and Wednesday night had to be a real drain, and so the church brought in musical guests for the occasional Sunday night program.

I loved these evenings, filled with new faces and songs both familiar and not. The altar call was replaced by a simple hymn of fellowship. We still had the offering, but instead of the regular kind, it was a Love Offering to help pay the musical guest's expenses in traveling to our fair town. I stole a sideways glance at Dad, hoping he'd throw in a dollar or two for the poor guest, who I'd imagine thumbing for a ride back to wherever he or she hailed from.

I hardly ever looked at my watch during these services, because unless the musical guest was irredeemably boring, she almost always beat out another exposition of Paul's letter to the church at Colossae.

One musical guest was a Korean lady who sang and played the piano. She was blind and deaf, kind of like a more talented version of Helen Keller. From the moment she walked over to the piano and began "How Great Thou Art," full of rolling arpeggios and trills that covered the entire keyboard, I was hooked. I played piano, and I could appreciate the years it had surely taken to do that, even with all one's senses intact. To do it blind and deaf was unimaginably fine.

Then, she sang Mozart's "Alleluia." I crossed and uncrossed my legs. My nose was tingling. My eyes watered, and I had to swallow three or four times, because it was just so … *wonderful* that anyone could make music like that, whether or not she could see or hear or smell or taste or touch.

My favorite musical guests ever were the Murks. Just like Halley's Comet, the Murk family returned with some regularity. The family consisted of the parents and their teenage children, Bill, Beverly, Brenda, Becky, and Barbara.

What did I *not* love about the Murks? They were beautiful, and the girls always wore cute mini dresses that I will admit to coveting. They also had shiny white go-go boots and long, long blonde hair. The girls were like real live Barbies, and Bill was like a Ken doll, blonde and buff. The analogy was perfect down to the smallest detail, for there were four Barbies to the one lone Ken.

They sang beautifully, all in harmony, and when they started "Heaven Came Down," glory did indeed fill my soul. Just when I thought they couldn't get any better, they each whipped out a violin and played those too. I just sat there and shook my head, because when Jesus said *Be ye therefore perfect, even as your Father which is in heaven is perfect,* the Murks had gone and taken it literally.

After the service, musical guests always offered tapes and records for sale at a table in the carport. Jill and I looked beseechingly at Dad. Could we *please* buy a record? As good frugal Germans, my parents weren't in the habit of making frivolous purchases for us, but records of Christian musical guests were usually deemed a worthy indulgence.

So Jill and I sneaked down the hall after the service. I gripped a five-dollar bill in my sweaty hand, careful not to lose it. We shyly approached the edge of the sales table, trying our best to avoid eye contact with the Murk family members manning the sales. They were gods, and if they should say something to me, I thought I would probably die right on the spot.

Our record choice depended on how much we liked the family's outfits on the cover. I voted for the one where the girls all wore red mini skirts, white go-go boots, and white coats with fur hoods. Jill preferred the one with the girls in powder blue maxi dresses.

Mom walked up, and decided on an 8-track tape featuring the coveted mini skirts. We had just gotten a new Ethan Allen dry sink that housed a record player and an 8-track tape player behind its doors; it was a wondrous thing. Our entire collection of 8-track tapes would forever be Elvis's Greatest Hits and the Murk family's "It's a Wonderful Way to Live."

Next Sunday night, I knew, we'd be back to hearing exhortations to the Colossians. But for tonight, I was happy to shove a wrinkled bill into Brenda Murk's hand. She smiled at me with gleaming white teeth and handed me my 8-track tape.

"Enjoy," she said.

It was kind of like a benediction.

Chapter 17 – Blessed Be the Name

Oh, for a thousand tongues to sing,
Blessed be the Name of the Lord!
The glories of my God and king!
Blessed be the Name of the Lord!

I held President Nixon in higher regard than most of the other chief executives I'd heard tell of, owing to the fact that I had actually seen him, even if it was only for about ten seconds. When I was six, Nixon had visited his mother's birthplace in the nearby town of Vernon, and our family had loaded up the car to witness him ride by in a parade. Mom managed to snag a photo that includes his head and outstretched arm, pointing at someone in the crowd as his car passed by. This was truly a miracle, as our family scrapbooks were full of photos of various folks who had been decapitated by the camera, even though they had stood totally still when the picture was taken.

I'll always remember the night President Nixon resigned. It was a typically humid August evening, and having been tipped off by Mom that this was an Event to Remember, I planned to commemorate it appropriately. My days in 4-H had cast a powerful spell, and I figured the best way to remember such an event was to create a personalized sewing project.

I dug out the pinking shears and cut a fabric rectangle, upon which I planned to embroider "President Nixon," underneath that a fish, and finally at the very bottom "August 8, 1974." I would keep it forever.

Being nine, I didn't understand much of what had happened to cause this resignation, but I knew that it involved somebody breaking into the Watergate. My parents had informed me that the Watergate was a hotel, but in my mind it was a sparkling body of water that featured a large grate through which water constantly flowed. Whenever I saw Watergate written in the newspaper, which was often, I'd picture that cool, flowing water, and I'd feel momentarily refreshed.

The family gathered in the family room to watch this historic happening. Unfortunately, President Nixon didn't speak long enough, because all I was able to finish on my project was the fish and PRES. I was distracted by the emotion of the moment, and by watching the president's wife, Pat, standing behind him. She looked so sad, yet she was holding it together so well. My heart went out to her, and I felt that she must be German.

Having finished his speech, Nixon got up to leave. I got up as well, setting my embroidery project onto a side table for another day.

"Gosh," I said, and that's all I got out before Mom stepped over and slapped me across the face.

This shocked me so much that I fell back a few feet into my chair.

"Why did you do that?" I asked, totally perplexed.

"We do NOT use God's name in vain in this family!" she said, leaning toward me with a truly frightening look on her face.

And now, I was feeling more hurt emotionally than physically. My own mom actually thought I would use God's name in vain? How could the woman who bore me know me so little? Because that was one thing I would never, ever do.

***

We learned the Ten Commandments young at First Baptist. Most of them were easy enough to keep -- I wasn't planning on worshiping an idol, murdering, or committing adultery (even though I wasn't totally sure what adultery meant; the fact that "adult" was its root word told me that it wasn't anything I had to worry about). I was a little iffy on coveting, particularly if it counted lusting after white go-go boots, a muff, or a station wagon, but I could keep that under control.

But one commandment I took especially seriously: *You shall not take the name of the Lord your God in vain, for the Lord will not hold him guiltless who takes his name in vain.*

Now *there* was a commandment you could sink your teeth into. It was specific, and really, it wasn't that difficult to keep if you just made up your mind to do it.

In our house, God's name was never taken in vain. Ever. No casual "Oh my g--" or "Oh g--!" for us.

Aunt Phyllis taught us in Rosebuds that it was even wrong to say "gosh" or "golly" as those were short for "God," or "gee" as that was short for "Jesus." Thus limited, it became quite a challenge to find appropriate exclamations. I resorted to "Oh, boogers!" as my go-to phrase for negative events, and "Oh, wow!" for almost everything else.

Duly chastened by Mom, I grabbed my pillow and headed down with the family to the living room for the night. It was one of those evenings so humid that we stopped trying to pretend that the attic fan was making any difference, and we all just camped out on the cooler ground-level living room floor. We left the front door open, and watched lightning bugs bounce off the screen door. It had been a humbling night for both President Nixon and me. He had lost the Presidency. I had learned the importance of good enunciation.

Chapter 18 – Onward, Christian Soldiers

Onward, Christian soldiers, marching as to war,
with the cross of Jesus going on before.
Christ, the royal Master, leads against the foe;
forward into battle see his banners go!

Onward, Christian soldiers, marching as to war,
with the cross of Jesus going on before.

There hadn't been so much excitement among the Wednesday night church kids since the last ice cream social: we were going to be soldiers! Christian soldiers, that is. Each week, we would learn about one piece of a Christian soldier's armor, and then create our own version. After a couple of months, we could don the whole armor of Christ and put on a little show for our parents, presumably making battle formations or doing some marching drills.

As the weeks passed, I eyed my growing collection of armor. My shield of faith had a nifty loop on the back, the better to hold it with. My helmet of salvation, fashioned from a plastic milk carton spray-painted gold, was uncomfortable yet impressive. The belt of truth had almost proved to be my undoing, with its intricate layers of felt appendages all held on with brads. And my feet were beautifully shod with the preparation of the gospel of peace, in tribute to the volunteer who'd designed a lace-up faux leather legging design for each of us to construct.

There exists a photo of me fully regaled in my armor. I've got on my helmet of salvation, my breastplate of righteousness, my belt of truthfulness, shoes of readiness, sword of the spirit, and I wrap up the look with my shield of faith, which let me extinguish all the devil's fiery darts.

In the photo, I hardly appear to be a battle commander's first pick. I'm a bit tentative, my chin tilted down, with a decidedly ambivalent look on my face. But maybe that's true for a lot of soldiers.

As I grew up in the fear and admonition of the Lord, I indeed felt that I was a Christian soldier. I was ready to fight, but the difficulty came in correctly identifying the enemy. After all, I'd learned my struggle was *not against flesh and blood, but against principalities, against powers, against the rulers of the darkness of this world, against spiritual wickedness in high places.*

That was enough to put any soldier on guard.

Sometimes, the enemy seemed pretty clear. Mom told me about Rhoda's older brother, Charlie. Charlie was in high school, and it seems that his science teacher had insisted that the class write papers on evolution. But Charlie stood up for Jesus, writing his essay on creationism instead and taking his "F" like a good Christian soldier.

I was impressed. I wanted to get good grades, and I wondered, when I reached high school, whether I'd be brave enough (and godly enough) to write about Adam and Eve having dinosaurs for pets, even when I knew it could sink me academically.

My years at First Baptist prepared me for other enemies as well. Our Wednesday night class met once in a simulation of the underground church, made up of Christians in countries where Christianity was not welcome. We turned off all the lights in the room and huddled in a corner with flashlights, whispering Bible verses to each other in the darkness and waiting for the pagan authorities to burst in at any moment.

I shivered, because I knew that this could become my reality, if America continued down its current path of denying Jesus. In 1963, the year prior to my birth, Madalyn Murray O'Hair won a lawsuit against Baltimore Public Schools, declaring prayer in public schools to be unconstitutional. It seemed that meeting as an underground church might not be far behind.

All the Sunday school teacher training manuals must have included a lesson involving the choice between Jesus and death, because it seemed to pop up every year. If our nation totally went down the toilet and descended into anarchy, how would I respond if a nameless authority asked me whether or not I was a Christian -- at gunpoint (it was always at gunpoint)?

This scenario scared me to death, to the extent that I could almost feel the gun's cold steel against my temple. Would I have the courage to bravely declare my allegiance to Christ, even if it meant getting my brains blown out? Would it maybe, just possibly, be acceptable to lie with my fingers crossed? Would Jesus understand that I really *did* love and claim him, and that I just wanted a little longer on planet earth?

I wasn't a bit sure I could get away with such a plan, though, because I knew the verse where Jesus said that *whosoever shall deny me before men, him will I also deny before my Father which is in heaven.* That didn't sound too promising, and I tried to push the whole scenario from my mind. Smoking and drinking were beginning to sound like small beans in the world of enemies, and even a Christian soldier needed to go on leave now and then.

***

It is required in ushers, that one knows how to wink.

I stood in my standard spot at the end of the pew, making circles on the floor with my shoe while Dr. Silver prayed the offertory prayer. I looked up at the usher standing in the aisle next to me, and he winked. Always, always, no matter who was ushering that night, he winked. I winked back, or I should say I tried to wink, because I was never totally successful at it. I could close one eye, but only if I also scrunched up that entire side of my face.

And just as I was unscrunching my face that night, the most piercing, other-earthly scream I'd ever heard sounded. It was shrill, and horrible. It went on and on, and goosebumps popped up all over my arms because I'd never heard anything like it. It didn't even sound like a human, and yet it had to be.

The entire congregation turned to find the source, and there it was, in the back center pew: a woman I'd never seen before, her face contorted.

"Amen," Dr. Silver wrapped up immediately, and Reverend Anderson, the minister of music, moved in quickly to make the best of the situation.

"Let's turn to a hymn of comfort, 'Leaning on the Everlasting Arms,'" he said, and we'd never turned to a hymn so quickly or so gratefully.

A large group of deacons surrounded the woman, and a few brave ones offered to counsel her in an empty Sunday school room.

The service continued, but I couldn't tell you a thing from the sermon. My teeth were chattering and I could not make them stop. The thought of that awful scream haunted me. I heard it over and over. How could a person make such a sound? And if a person couldn't … where had it come from?

After the service, the congregants gathered to whisper in small groups. I heard the phrase "demon possessed!" piping up from the conversations, and it terrified me. Demons were in the Bible, sure. I knew about the demons that had entered that herd of swine and made them run off the cliff. But people being demon possessed? Right now, in Seymour? At my church? Balaam's donkey might as well have showed up and started talking, because that seemed just about as likely.

But my teeth kept knocking against each other, and I watched like a hawk for talking donkeys, stray demons, or anything else that might be just around the corner.

***

I loved going to Miriam's for the night. We'd make no-bake cookies and drink Tang, and then we'd spend the entire afternoon playing the Game of Life. I didn't have the Game of Life at my house, and the little blue and pink people in the cars captivated me. After living out our lives in game form, we headed outside to walk her dog around the neighborhood. When it was time for bed, we both climbed into Miriam's great big bed, much bigger than my twin-size one.

My eyelids drooped within minutes of hitting the sheets, but Miriam was always eager to read me stories about the Bermuda Triangle, the lost city of Atlantis, or her hero, Jacques Cousteau. I envied Miriam because she knew exactly what she wanted to be when she grew up: either an oceanographer or a marine biologist. The only career aspiration I had was to be a Mousketeer.

Miriam's slumber party began much the same way. Our little group played Battleship to our heart's content before heading down to the basement, where we engaged in several rounds of truth or dare. We were all hoping that Sally would fall asleep first, because she'd told us she was a heavy sleeper. Nothing, apparently, would awaken her. Miriam had heard that if you put someone's hand into a bowl of water while they were sleeping, they would pee their pants. We thought it would be just hilarious to test this theory out, and Sally seemed to be the ideal candidate. But she didn't appear to be getting very tired, so Miriam pulled out the Very Embarrassing, fully illustrated "Facts of Life" book she'd sneaked off the bookshelf in her parents' room. We giggled and squealed over each page.

"Hey," Laurie said, after we'd exhausted the number of times we could page through the most embarrassing parts, "I brought a Ouija board!"

"Cool!" came the whispered chorus. Because while the "Facts of Life" book was pretty grown-up, the Ouija board trumped it, by a lot.

And right then the uncomfortable thought occurred to me that I was going to need to put on my Christian armor, because while I didn't know much of anything about a Ouija board, I did know that it was wrong.

Thankfully, Cyndy put words to my thoughts.

"What exactly do you do with a Ouija board?"

"You put your hands on the marker in the middle." Laurie explained this like one who had done it many times. "Then, you close your eyes, and think of a question, and your hands will move to letters that spell out the answer."

Cyndy frowned. "What's so amazing about that?"

Laurie grinned, because this was her gotcha moment: "*You* don't move your hands! The spirit does!"

In my mind, I'd already donned my helmet of salvation, and I was reaching for the breastplate of righteousness, because I knew that the spirit in question here wasn't the Holy one. Dr. Silver had just recently preached about evil spirits, and how they traveled through dry places, looking for rest. I figured, wouldn't it be just my luck if the girls scared up a spirit who'd come and choose me for permanent residence? Closing my eyes and remembering that screaming woman in church, I wanted to get far, far away.

But apparently no one else had any reservations, and they gathered expectantly around the board with Laurie in the dimly lit room.

Cyndy and I fled the scene and sat on the wooden steps leading up to the kitchen. Apparently, we were fellow soldiers in this battle.

"I don't wanna play with a Ouija board," she said, looking miserable.

"Me either," I admitted, and we sat in silence and darkness for a little while, watching light emanate from the room where the others were learning various things, from who their first boyfriends would be to the names of their future children.

"I think we should pray for them," Cyndy whispered finally, and I agreed. So we sat on the steps, praying that our friends wouldn't be struck dead for calling on evil spirits. Then we began talking, and found that we had a lot in common. We both were the oldest kids in our families. We both liked rabbits. We both had a penchant for *I Love Lucy* and *The Carol Burnett Show.*

A few hours later, or maybe it was just ten minutes, Miriam's mom opened the door and almost tripped over us.

"What are you girls doing out here?" she asked, full of concern. We explained our aversion to the Ouija board, and she was sympathetic, although she didn't make the others stop playing.

"How about if you just come up and visit in the kitchen?" she suggested, and we agreed that this was a fine idea.

So it was that I came to see that fellow Christian soldiers can rise up anywhere, and at the most unexpected of times. They didn't all go to First Baptist.

Chapter 19 – Count Your Blessings

When upon life's billows you are tempest-tossed,
When you are discouraged, thinking all is lost,
Count your many blessings – name them one by one,
And it will surprise you what the Lord has done.
Count your blessings – name them one by one;
Count your blessings – see what God has done!
Count your blessings – name them one by one;
Count your many blessings – see what God has done.

I wanted nothing more than a baton when I was eight. Maybe I'd just seen a few too many majorettes strutting past in the local parades, but I was convinced that a baton was the only thing I lacked for a successful future.

So when I spied one, gleaming on top of my Christmas pile of gifts, my joy was great. Mom signed me up for baton class, and on Tuesday after school I hopped onto the Girls Club bus. I spent the entire ride with my eyes closed, imagining myself in a sparkly leotard on stage, twirling my baton with zest and throwing it up into the air over and over, catching it perfectly each time. I was graceful and beautiful, kind of like a dancer, but baton twirling was not the same as dancing, and therefore it was just fine morally.

I peered hesitantly into the huge Girls Club gym, full of girls my age with similar batons. Jonra, our instructor, was a terribly cool teenager with long wavy hair and a psychedelic poncho that I would die for. I had a poncho my grandma had crocheted for me, but it was only red and white.

"Okay. This is baton class, and I just have one rule: you aren't allowed to say 'I can't.' Got it?" She popped her gum and walked among us.

Standing on my spot marked with a masking tape X, I learned the first move, chocolate and vanilla. This involved dipping one end of the baton down and then dipping the other end down, in a swirly kind of way. It was easy.

Then we moved on to regular twirling, which was a little harder, but not much. That was the last skill I was able to master. Jonra asked us to do a fancy move, which involved sliding the baton over a couple of our fingers, and I found it impossible.

I raised my hand.

Jonra walked over and momentarily stopped doing the move with her own baton.

"I …" Uh oh. I wasn't allowed to say 'I can't,' but I was unsure how to phrase it any other way.

"I … am not able to do that," I said.

Jonra rolled her eyes and began effortlessly flicking her baton around again. When I tried to copy her, it just wasn't the same.

She shrugged. "Just keep doing chocolate and vanilla," she offered, before returning to the front of class.

Our group performed a routine to "March of the Toy Soldiers" for the final class, and I was competent for approximately 30 seconds of the two-minute song. Several of those seconds involved dipping my knees and tapping the end of the baton on the ground while the baby-voiced girl on the record sang *Oompah, Oompah.*

But I twirled, chocolate-and-vanillaed, and oompahed with pride, there in the back row. I looked out at Mom, Dad, and Jill, all smiling, and I knew that this baton had indeed been a step in the right direction for me.

***

Standing in the hazy sunshine of the outfield, I prayed the baseball wouldn't come anywhere near me. This was P.E. class, and I wasn't any more successful at sports than I'd been at baton. Because of this, I was always assigned the outfield position, although I didn't mind. In fact, my biggest fear was that the ball would approach me and I might actually have to attempt catching it.

P.E. classes began at my school when I was in fourth grade, and they became my thorn in the flesh. Each year when the gym teacher announced the Presidential Fitness Test trial, I knew it was only a question of how badly I'd fail to reach minimum standards this time. Only "effort" raised my "F" grades in various sports to D-minuses.

But as I stood in the outfield, swatting at mosquitoes and twisting my hair, a strange and wonderful thing happened. Bible verses popped into my mind. Hymns, too, and the funny thing was that they were always what I needed in that moment. "Count Your Blessings" became my baseball song, and I found that concentrating on my blessings helped me avoid concentrating on my athletic shortcomings.

All those years of memorizing verses, of singing hymns, and of falling asleep at night while Mom practiced Sunday's hymns on the piano downstairs had cemented them into my brain, and now they came back to me at the most opportune times, almost like a sixth sense. They were as much a part of me as my brown hair, my nearsighted eyes, and my ever, ever wondering mind.

Thus the great hymns and verses of consolation became my therapy. They spoke to my soul, and soothed me when nothing else would.

***

"Today in class, I've set up an obstacle course," Mr. Drummond, the P.E. teacher, announced. I liked Mr. Drummond, or I should say I wanted to like him, because in my mind the categories P.E. Teachers and People I Like were mutually exclusive. But had he not taught P.E., his easy-going manner and his big smile would have appealed to me.

His obstacle course did not.

"First, you'll run from this end of the gym to the other. Then, I've set up some hurdles for you to jump. After that, there's a tumbling section where you'll do two backwards somersaults and a vault before finishing up with a cartwheel. We'll go three at a time. Don't fiddle faddle around, because I'll be timing you. If you take longer than three minutes, I'm putting your name on the Twinkie list!"

He walked to the chalkboard and wrote TWINKIE LIST in large letters at the top.

I swallowed, three or four times actually, but prepared to give the course my best shot. When it was my turn, I did well on the running part. I fell behind the other two kids on hurdles, but my performance still wasn't awful. But then, the backwards somersaults sealed my doom. I hated backwards somersaults. I had been graded on them before, and I'd gotten a big ol' F because I just could not get my body to go back over my head. Mom had issued Dad an anguished plea: "Can't you *please* help that child do a backwards somersault?" Dad had dutifully spent an evening trying to shove me over, time after time. But once he left, I was hopeless.

And so, my competitors moved on and finished while I remained on the mat, wracked with humiliation as I tried rolling back over my head again, and again, and again. Some of the other kids snickered, and finally Mr. Drummond shouted, "Okay, just go ahead to the vault."

As I finished, he walked to the board and wrote my name on the Twinkie List. The only other kid listed was Chuck, the class clown, and everybody knew he had just gone slow on purpose.

My eyes began to burn and my nose felt weird as well. I knew I was *this close* to crying, and yet I would rather die than look like a bawl baby in P.E. class.

I grabbed mentally for any trick to console me.

I like Twinkies! Especially the cream part -- yum! It's not so bad to be on the Twinkie List. It's just a joke ...

Not helping.

But then, my sixth sense kicked in.

By and by, when the morning comes,
when the saints of God are gathered home,
we'll tell the story how we've overcome,
for we'll understand it better by and by.

I could hear the tune in my head, and it comforted me. Oh, could I ever imagine telling the story of how I overcame the Twinkie List to all those saints in glory one of these days. I got into line at the end of gym class, grateful beyond all get out to be heading back to the classroom, where I knew my name would never appear on any Twinkie List.

Life could be confusing and unfair at times, that was for sure. But I'd understand it better by and by.

Chapter 20 – All the Way My Savior Leads Me

All the way my Savior leads me, what have I to ask beside?
Can I doubt His tender mercy, who through life has been my Guide?
Heav'nly peace, divinest comfort, here by faith in Him to dwell!
For I know, whate'er befall me, Jesus doeth all things well;
For I know, whate'er befall me, Jesus doeth all things well.

My three great childhood wishes were a pair of go-go boots, a muff, and a station wagon. On vacations especially, I fervently wished for a station wagon, since our vacations always seemed to involve lengthy car rides. I felt that station wagons were the ultimate luxury travel item, and I loved their every aspect from the wood side paneling to the large back compartment, where I imagined Jill and me spreading out our Fisher Price Little People and playing as we sped along, mile after mile.

But a station wagon never materialized for our family, and so Jill and I passed the hours locating all the letters of the alphabet on road signs, over and over and over, in the family sedan. We also colored pictures, read books, and mercilessly insisted on sneaking various body parts over onto the other's side of the backseat until Dad dubbed the center segment "no man's land." Looking up into the rear-view mirror, he vowed, "Enough of this orneriness. Next person to cross over into No Man's Land will get her fanny tanned!"

We knew this was no idle threat. Time-outs were unknown in our house, and my dad's job as a school principal had given him plenty of practice tanning hides. More than once, he'd pulled the car over along the roadside and broken a branch from a nearby tree, the better to tan our fannies with. I found this highly humiliating, and so I got my act together in short order.

Singing as we made our way along the highway was popular as well, and Jill and I loved singing "Plant a Watermelon Over My Grave (and let the juice – slurp, slurp – sift through)," and sometimes the edgy "99 Bottles of Beer on the Wall."

The only song I ever heard Dad sing was "How Much is that Doggie in the Window?" He sang this in a modified monotone, packing most of his effort into the "arf arf"'s at the end of each phrase. Mom maintained that once, years ago, a music teacher had told Dad that he could have a real nice voice if he had some training. But that training never came, and so the doggie song remained his entire repertoire.

As dusk arrived, we began our search for a decent, yet inexpensive, motel. Once we found one, Jill and I marveled at every detail of the room, from the pictures above the beds to the plush and exotic carpeting to the layout of the bathroom. One time we convinced Dad to let us use a quarter to activate the bed's "Magic Fingers." I lay on the bed, expecting an otherworldly, magical experience. When the bed merely rattled for three minutes before resuming its inert state, my disappointment was profound.

***

I opened my eyes to a new day, and saw Mom and Dad huddled around the motel phone book, thumbing through the yellow pages. And then, with a twisting of my stomach, it hit me: this was Sunday, and where could I flee from God's presence? Nowhere, because we were going to church, here on vacation. Here in a town I'd never set foot in before.

I knew that we needed to honor the Sabbath Day by keeping it holy. I just wished that that didn't involve going to church with a bunch of strangers. Yet whenever a vacation day fell on a Sunday, Mom and Dad found a church and off we went. And we didn't just go to the service -- oh no, we did the whole nine yards. We went to Sunday school, too.

***

We pulled into the local Baptist church parking lot, and I gazed up at the tall white steeple. What adventures would await me this morning?

"We have a ten year old and a seven year old," Mom informed the friendly deacon who greeted us at the door.

"Oh, well, let me introduce you to our Sunday school superintendent!" This jolly older man led us down a series of hallways, where I was eventually dropped off at a room with a circle of small wooden chairs. I took a seat, trying not to stare at the other two girls and boy already in attendance. There was no teacher as yet, and so the four of us were companions in an awkward silence.

When the teacher finally arrived, she was the soul of enthusiasm: "Boys and girls, we have a guest! This is Susan! She lives in Indiana!"

The boy spoke. "Does it snow there?" He didn't ask this to me, but to the teacher. I supposed I was just a museum exhibit of sorts, 'Susan from Indiana.'

"Does it?" the teacher asked me, and I could see the relief in her eyes when I answered, "Yes."

The kids all looked at me admiringly. I was happy to have some claim to fame, even if it had come through no effort on my part.

***

I sat gratefully in the sanctuary, having survived Sunday school. I was now blessedly reunited with my family. The church service felt pretty familiar, and it was an odd comfort to realize that Baptist preachers everywhere must like to bless "the words of our mouths and the meditations of our hearts," even in Florida.

Then the preacher gave the announcement that I knew was coming.

"If you're visiting with us today, we're just thrilled to have you here. If you'd just signal to the ushers stationed in the aisles, they'd love to give you a welcome packet that you can fill out and a little gift to take home with you."

I looked at Dad in alarm. Would he raise his hand for a packet, thereby again drawing attention to us, and perhaps even triggering an introduction to the whole congregation? I could imagine the preacher asking Mom and Dad if it snowed in Indiana, or whether we grew corn in the backyard, or even if they'd like to suggest a hymn to sing. It would be so embarrassing!

But Dad sat in the pew, still as a stone. During the church service, at least, we would remain anonymous, and I breathed a sigh of relief for our German heritage.

Chapter 21 – The Great Physician

The Great Physician now is near,
The sympathizing Jesus;
He speaks the drooping heart to cheer,
Oh, hear the voice of Jesus.

Sweetest note in seraph song,
Sweetest name on mortal tongue,
Sweetest carol ever sung,
Jesus, blessed Jesus!

Pretty and smart. As a girl, I figured those were my two basic categories in which to excel. Smart I had down fairly well, but pretty I was struggling with.

One obstacle was my solid build, resulting no doubt from my being German. I wasn't fat, but I was chubby enough that people's first instinct upon seeing me was to comment on how pretty my face was. The problem with this was that my face wasn't especially pretty. I wished for long, wavy curls to at least help me out a little in the facial beauty department, but Mom vetoed this. For years, she directed Mrs. Stout, a First Baptist member who cut our hair in her home studio, to trim my hair in a short bob, which she optimistically termed a pixie cut. "It's easy to take care of," Mom would say enthusiastically, as if this would convince me of the style's merits. Further, Mom swore it made me look like Dorothy Hamill, but I wasn't buying that. I thought it just made me look like a boy, and more than once I was mistaken for one, to my great consternation.

I also suffered in comparison to my sister Jill, who was dainty and often even sickly. Mom loved to tout that I, by contrast, was *healthy as an ox!* I had a mental image of oxen, and it wasn't pretty. They were boxy and slow, and they ate grass. I did not aspire to be one of them.

The size of my feet was another trial. Each fall, Mom took me downtown to Stahl's Shoe Store for new school shoes. And each year, I'd look at the cute shoes displayed on little plastic boxes set among a fall display featuring pine cones, fake leaves, and piles of school books. I'd choose the pair I liked most, if it was in our price range, and then I'd sit down and wait for reality to hit. For when the shoe salesman returned with the shoes in my size, they bore no resemblance whatsoever to the cute footwear I'd seen on display. No, the shoes in my size looked more like boats. Their great size removed any visual appeal they'd originally possessed, and although I dutifully sat while the salesman tied them onto my feet, my enthusiasm was gone.

"Do you like them?" Mom would ask. "Because I don't want you to act like you like them here, and then we get them home and you won't wear them." She rolled her eyes and shrugged apologetically to the salesman. Then she'd launch into the Shoe Speech, which I had memorized: "Big feet are nothing to be ashamed of! Big feet give you a good foundation! You're probably going to be a big person!" Well, that was encouraging.

What could I say? *I like the shoes on the display, but in my size, they're ugly!* I didn't want to hurt the salesman's feelings by criticizing the shoes, but the fact remained: the shoes he had put onto my feet were not cute. I did not like them. And yet, I couldn't go to school barefoot. So each year, this strange dance occurred, and each year it ended with us bringing home a box of large, ugly shoes which I proceeded to wear to school each day, like a good girl.

My healthy constitution made me one of the tallest and largest girls in my class each year, consigned to the back row for class pictures and the back riser for church programs. How I longed to be one of the petite girls in the front row, looking so tiny and cute! Instead, I was reliably placed in the back, often next to the teacher, where my solid form made a sturdy visual anchor for the group. Dad called me "Big Sue," and with a nickname like that, I figured life could only improve.

But it wouldn't improve right away. A visit to the eye doctor in third grade revealed a further insult: I was quite near-sighted, and needed glasses.

"Why didn't you tell us you couldn't see?" Mom asked, while Dad expressed my thinking: "Maybe she thought everybody saw like she did."

I was now not only a big girl, who shopped for clothes in the Chubbies department (at least the larger boys got the more positively-spun "Husky Town"), but I had glasses as well. I sat in the optometrist's waiting room, tears quietly rolling down my cheeks.

"You get new glasses!" Mom enthused, waving her hands. "You can even pick out the frames! Aren't you excited?"

No, I was not, and I knew that no amount of Love's Baby Soft would distract people from my extra set of eyes.

I had only a few short years to adjust to these misfortunes before Mom marched me to the orthodontist. I didn't have a good feeling about this, suspecting that Dr. Clark had never seen a mouth he couldn't improve. Sure enough, he recommended braces.

This was too much.

In my room, I contemplated the monstrosity that I would soon become: a chubby girl, with glasses and braces. I was ugly as sin. How could one girl handle this much adversity?

And then, I caught the eye of Jesus, hanging in portrait version on my wall since the day I'd won him in Miss Harrington's class. Jesus was the great physician. Surely he had borne my sorrows. He wouldn't give me more than I could bear. He could do anything, even bring people back from the dead. Was it too much to ask him to straighten my teeth? They weren't even *that* crooked, although that wasn't the point. I had faith to believe he could fix my teeth even if they looked like the stalactites and stalagmites in Wyandotte Cave!

I decided to pray about this. After all, I'd learned to pray without ceasing. Bring every concern before God. I hadn't bothered Jesus with too many selfish requests, as this surely was, and I sincerely hoped he'd answer me with a 'green light.'

So I launched into the most fervent prayer of my life thus far, summoning up all the faith I could: *Dear Jesus, please make my teeth straight. You know that I'm already fat. I already have glasses. I just don't think I can face life with braces too. I know you can do it, Jesus, so please ...*

I inched over to the lighted makeup mirror on my dresser and slowly opened my mouth.

I was crushed to see that the gap between my front teeth remained. Why hadn't Jesus answered me? Didn't I have enough faith to believe? I totally believed that Jesus *could* straighten my teeth. I guessed my failure had come from a lack of faith that he *would.*

Further thought led me to the inescapable conclusion: Jesus was indeed going to straighten my teeth, but apparently he planned for Dr. Clark to be his tool in that venture.

The Bible said *if ye have faith as a grain of mustard seed, ye shall say unto this mountain, Remove hence to yonder place; and it shall remove.*

Faith the size of a mustard seed, the tiniest of all seeds, could move a mountain. I didn't want to know how small my faith was, if it couldn't even move a set of teeth.

Chapter 22 – What if it Were Today?

Jesus is coming to earth again; what if it were today?
Coming in power and love to reign; what if it were today?
Coming to claim His chosen Bride, all the redeemed and purified,
Over this whole earth scattered wide; what if it were today?
Glory, glory! Joy to my heart 'twill bring.
Glory, glory! When we shall crown Him King.
Glory, glory! Haste to prepare the way;
Glory, glory! Jesus will come some day.

I feared two things as a child: the scale, and Jesus' return.

Twice each year at Jackson Elementary, Mrs. Slade, the school secretary, weighed each child. She would pull the big scale from the health room down the hall and into each classroom, and she'd park it up front at the teacher's desk. Then our teacher called out our names, one by one, and Mrs. Slade weighed us, calling out our weight so the teacher could write it onto our report cards.

It didn't take long to figure out that the fatter you were, the softer Mrs. Slade announced your weight. We kids were all wise to this, and you could have heard a pin drop when the weights were being called out. Even though I detested being weighed myself, I couldn't resist remembering a few unbelievable statistics as they wafted past my ears: Tom weighed 150! Tonda weighed 127!

I probably weighed ten pounds more than the average girl in my class, but in my mind it might as well have been 100. Miriam, being a girl of size like me, shared my outrage at the injustice of public weighing, and we spent many a recess discussing this. Did the teacher read each kid's IQ aloud twice each year? No! It just wasn't fair! And we reported any suspicious rattling sounds we'd heard in the hallway that morning: could it have been the scale, traveling to a classroom just down the hall? Because if it was, our classroom could be next!

We brainstormed every possible way to avoid this humiliating spectacle, without success. The only way to get out of it was to be sick on weighing day. Those lucky kids were sent to the health room upon their return, to be weighed in blessed seclusion. The problem with planning a sick day, though, was that no one knew the day or the hour when the scale would roll down the hall. It was a dilemma.

***

Jesus: he was my best friend, although we'd never met. But that would change, because I knew that one of these days, Jesus was coming back. The Second Coming was a favorite topic of Dr. Silver's, but it was usually reserved for Sunday night services. This was hardly surprising, since a quick glance through Revelation would be enough to scare away any poor heathen who might have wandered into a Sunday morning church service.

It seemed that Dr. Silver preached about Revelation almost every Sunday night of my youth. Over and over he warned us not to be like the Laodiceans, who were lukewarm, or *carnal*. If I made a Top Ten list of words Dr. Silver used in sermons, carnal would no doubt reside near the top. Carnality was to be avoided at all costs, and I feared I might be sliding into it without meaning to. Where was the dividing line? If I skipped a day of Bible reading, did that count as carnal? What about repeatedly falling asleep while praying? I felt it was vital to know, because the stakes were high. As Exhibit A of carnality, the Laodiceans were going to be spewed out of Jesus' mouth. I spent many a slice of childhood contemplating this. Was he really going to spew them out, or was this figurative? Neither option was good.

But spewing was mild compared to the rest of Revelation and the terrors Dr. Silver enumerated: the mark of the beast, the various plagues, and the blood-red moon. The pale white death stallion and the beast with seven heads were so *far out* that they were hard to imagine really existing, but the blood-red moon? Now there was an image that burned into my brain.

Rev 6:12 - And I beheld when he had opened the sixth seal, and, lo, there was a great earthquake; and the sun became black as sack-cloth of hair, and the moon became as blood.

After the service one night, I ambled out of church for my leisurely stroll to the family car. My mind pondered the lyrics to the evening's special music, "I Wish We'd All Been Ready."

Life was filled with guns and war,
And everyone got trampled on the floor,
I wish we'd all been ready,
Children died, the days grew cold,
A piece of bread could buy a bag of gold,
I wish we'd all been ready,
There's no time to change your mind,
How could you have been so blind,
The Father spoke, the demons dined,
The Son has come and you've been left behind.

I glanced skyward, and there it was: the moon was red! *Blood-red!* My own blood ran cold. If the moon was blood-red, that could only mean we were gearing up for the tribulation, that great and awful period just preceding Jesus' return.

Dr. Silver had taught us that during that time, only those with the mark of the beast would be able to buy food. And Christians wouldn't be allowed to get the mark of the beast, so .... I shuddered, contemplating slowly starving to death under the light of the bloody moon. If that weren't awful enough, things could become even worse, because another option for Christians during the tribulation was to die as martyrs. While I loved Jesus, I wasn't sure I had martyrdom in me.

I glanced up again. *Darn!* The moon still sported a swirly, sickeningly reddish appearance. I did a quick mental calculation. I was currently ten, so if the seven-year tribulation period began now, I'd only make it to age 17 (and I knew my odds were slim of being alive even that long, given what was coming).

I would never have a chance to go to college … get married … have kids … my mind began to panic. *Why couldn't I have been born maybe ten years earlier? At least then I'd have a few more years!*

At home later that night, my angst reached a point where I just had to share it with someone. I went into our bedroom and found Jill playing with her dolls. Being three years younger, she wasn't nearly as attentive to Dr. Silver's sermons as I was, and I felt it was my filial duty to share with her about the trying times to come.

"Jill."

"Yeah?" she kept rocking her doll, not even looking up at me. *Ignorance is bliss,* Mom always said, and I knew this to be unarguably true.

"I don't know if you've been listening to Dr. Silver, but he's been preaching about Revelation." I was trying to ease into this gently.

"So?" Now she was ironing clothes with her little pretend iron. *Ah, to be so young and carefree!* I thought. *She has no idea that soon we may be huddling together in the cold with other believers, probably people we don't even like, in an effort to ward off death for another day.*

"Well, it's pretty important stuff to know, since we're Christians. Revelation talks about the end times, and when those times come, which could be any day now, Christians are going to have it really bad. We won't be allowed to buy food. There are going to be beasts and dragons and a woman clothed with the sun, and horses that are red and pale, and scorpions with stingers that can't kill people, but they'll be so awful that people will be wishing to die …"

In my zeal, I had forgotten to gauge my audience's reaction. Jill had put down her baby and her ironing and was staring at me with a wide-eyed look of terror.

"When is that happening?" she gasped.

"No man knoweth the day or the hour," I said quietly, "but I heard Mom telling this on the phone. Her friend's friend was driving the other day. The friend saw a man walking along the road, and she stopped to pick him up. He said to her, 'Ma'am, I was sent to tell you that Gabriel's getting ready to blow his trumpet!'"

"What does that mean?"

"Well, Gabriel's an angel, so I would assume it means Jesus is about to come back. And then, the freakiest part is, the man turned away and didn't get into the car. When the friend drove off, she looked for him, and he had just disappeared!"

Jill had begun crying at this point, and I followed her as she fled down to the family room, where my dad was intensely involved with a basketball game on TV.

"Dad, Susan's telling me all this scary stuff that is going to happen! The world is going to end! Gabriel's going to blow his trumpet! We might starve! We might even get killed!"

Dad turned from his game with a perturbed look, bordering dangerously on anger. I'm not sure if this stemmed more from the subject at hand, or the interruption. Because if there was one thing that could override even Dad's German heritage, it was a good basketball game, or even, quite honestly, a bad one.

"Quit telling her stuff like that!" he said. "Everyone who likes Jesus is going to be okay."

He returned to his game.

Actually, I'm not so sure about that … I wanted to break in. *If you read Revelation, things might even be **worse** for the people who love Jesus, at least short-term.*

But I could see that he wasn't up for a debate on eschatology, and clearly my warning cry had not had the intended effect on my sister either. I supposed Jesus was right about a prophet having no honor in his own hometown.

I briefly wondered whether it was even worthwhile to brush my teeth that night, since my days might be cut tragically short.

Then again, there was the small chance that my dad might be right, and that everyone who liked Jesus would be okay.

In the end, I took my chances and squirted some Crest onto my toothbrush. Sometimes, you had to step out in faith.

Chapter 23 – Joy to the World

Joy to the World , the Lord is come!
Let earth receive her King;
Let every heart prepare Him room,
And Heaven and nature sing,
And Heaven and nature sing,
And Heaven, and Heaven, and nature sing.

Jill and I were glued to Schoolhouse Rock on the family room TV one spring morning when Mom walked in and closed the door behind her.

"Girls, I have something to tell you. I've never had to tell you anything like this before …" She paused.

I looked up from *Lolly, lolly, lolly, get your adverbs here*, because this wasn't Mom's standard operating procedure. She usually talked as she worked, multi-tasking up a storm. For her to enter a room, give us her full attention, and make a pronouncement was unheard of. I steeled myself for an announcement of terminal cancer and imagined myself as a motherless child, eating TV dinners for supper and spending most school nights at junior high basketball games. The adults there would all shake their heads and cluck their tongues in sympathy for me, and no doubt people would go out of their way to be nice to me, but still, it would be a burden.

"I'm going to have a baby," Mom announced, looking at us anxiously. Jill and I turned to each other in surprise, for this was surely an unexpected development. It had been just the two of us for seven years, and for three years prior to that it was only me. Sure, I'd walked the path to motherhood with Lucy when she had Little Ricky, and with Wilma Flintstone when she'd had Pebbles, but a baby in our house?

Later that week, I overheard mom confiding in her friend Ruby on the phone.

"I'm not sure how this happened," she whispered anxiously.

I wasn't either, because my mom was quite old – at least 33! I had no idea how she had ended up in this predicament at such an advanced age.

***

There are teachers I remember because of their ability to inspire me, and then there are teachers I remember for other reasons. Mr. Rueger, my fifth grade music teacher, fell into the second group. He liked to wear sweater vests, and he was as mild-mannered a man as I'd ever known. Perhaps that was why he gave up on our class early in the school year. Maybe it was due to excessive talking when he turned to move the needle on the record player, or maybe it was one too many paper airplanes sailing across the room, but Mr. Rueger stopped teaching us the lines of the treble clef and the meaning of *giocoso* and reverted to the music teacher's fall-back: the packet of song lyrics.

Each time we had music class, he handed out packets of lyrics to popular songs. The mimeographed sheets with their purple ink smelled good at first, but that quickly faded. Soon, the back sheets began to come unstapled and the pages were all creased. But we'd each clutch our copy, flipping through it in anticipation of the question we knew was coming.

"Alright then, boys and girls, what would you like to sing first today?" Mr. Rueger stared out at us serenely.

"Mack the Knife!" Chuck yelled, and we were off. Mr. Rueger dropped the needle, and we sang the whole song. "Mack the Knife" always confused me. Was Mack a shark, or a person? And the singing about the "body oozing life" always brought forth a chorus of "Ewwwww!" from the girls, and "Yeah!" from the boys, at least for the first few months we sang it.

Then it was on to "I'm On the Top of the World," "He Ain't Heavy, He's my Brother," and a slew of others. Mr. Rueger led us in singing them all, standing in front of the class and clutching his lyrics packet with one hand, the other resting on his ample stomach. Meanwhile, most of the class was joking, writing notes, or folding paper airplanes. A few of the braver ones even walked right up behind Mr. Rueger and gave him bunny ears.

But if he even noticed this, Mr. Rueger didn't bat an eye. He just kept singing.

As a good Christian girl, I wasn't about to blatantly misbehave. But Miriam and I rebelled on a small scale during "Bridge Over Troubled Water." We liked to put one arm in front of us as a bridge, and parade the fingers of our other hand across it in dramatic fashion. This seemed risky at the time.

"Susan and Miriam, I'd like to see you after class," Mr. Rueger said mildly as we filed out of the music room one November day.

We eyed each other with a distinctly bad feeling. Had he taken notice of our "Bridge Over Troubled Water" routine and disapproved? We stayed, eyeing each other warily.

"Well, girls, I'm planning our Christmas concert, and I'd like you two to sing a duet!" Mr. Rueger smiled and showed more enthusiasm and, well, *life*, than I'd known him to even possess.

"Here's the music. Miriam, why don't you take the soprano line and Susan, you can do the alto. I'll work with you at lunch recess starting next week."

And with that, he left. We walked down the hallway, unsure of what to even say. I supposed we didn't really have the option to tell Mr. Rueger no, but I had the lousy feeling that my good behavior had gotten me into a mess. It wasn't the first time, and it wouldn't be the last.

***

The night of the school program, Miriam and I stood together in the front row due to our duet. Under normal circumstances, a front row spot would have thrilled me beyond belief, but my nerves made gratitude impossible on this night. As the choir finished each number, Miriam and I squeezed each other's hand. One song closer to our duet!

When the moment came, we crossed the huge stage to the center microphone and began singing "Born to be King" in a quiet, yet sincere, way. We sang in unison, because Mr. Rueger had learned that good behavior didn't necessarily indicate an ability to sing in parts. I wore my new Christmas maxi dress from the Sears catalog. The fabric looked like quilt squares, and I thought it was beautiful.

" ...and that's how it was at the birth of the boy who's the cause of all joy, the boy who was born to be King!"

I looked over at Mr. Rueger, who was standing at the side of the stage with his hands clasped over his red sweater vest. He looked so pleased that it almost made up for the stress he'd put us through. Miriam and I took a brief, head-ducking bow, and returned to our spots on the risers.

***

First Baptist also put on a children's Christmas program. It wasn't anything as impressive as re-enacting the first Christmas, and it didn't even call for costumes. No, our production was more modest, with traditional Christmas carols and of course "parts."

Many kids were given speaking parts, and my faithful attendance usually scored me a big one.

Each night after supper, Mom and Dad would listen to me say my part, usually a four-line rhyme designed to draw an "Aww!" from the audience -- that is, if they could understand it.

Christmas, merry Christmas!
Is it really come again?
With its memories and greetings,
With its joys and with its pain

I was terribly conflicted over how to pronounce "again." Should I go with the traditional pronunciation? If so, what should I do with the fact that "pain" and "again" didn't rhyme? Or should I say "aGAIN" and sound ridiculous, yet preserve the rhyme? I considered asking our director, Mrs. Meyers, but she didn't appear to be too interested in the intricacies of the language in my part. Slow and loud were really all that mattered.

"Susan! Speak up and slow down, please!"

I tried again, mumbling "again" and "pain" so that hopefully listeners could hear what they wanted to, and was rewarded with a lackluster "okay, next!"

***

Christmas time was magical. Mom made a felt advent calendar that she hung on the paneled wall by the kitchen table, and we put up a little piece each day. I learned Christmas carols on the piano, playing through all the verses like we did at church. This had its rewards; I learned that holly bore a bark as bitter as any gall from the fifth verse of "The Holly and the Ivy." Our family gathered by the TV to watch all the Christmas specials, from Rudolph and Frosty to the Little Drummer Boy and Charlie Brown. I liked to sit in a large cardboard box with my stuffed Santa and pretend I was at the drive-in.

On Christmas Eve, we headed to church for the children's program. I made it through my part, and at the end of the service we all lined the sanctuary with our little candles, lit with help from a few strategically-placed deacons. These same candles made an appearance each Christmas, as evidenced by their shrinking size each year and their wax-stained paper holders.

Then the lights went out, and we sang, "Let there be Peace on Earth." Through the years, there were some anxious moments with the candles, from biggies like Laura briefly catching her hair on fire to smaller incidents like me burning my fingers on the scalding bits of dripping wax. Still, it was our tradition and it was comforting to see the peaceful glow and wonder if there really would be peace on earth someday. It wasn't too much to hope for, because everything seemed possible on Christmas Eve.

Jill and I followed Mom and Dad out the carport door, picking up boxes of Christmas candy that were lined up on a table just for the kids. The blue boxes featured the wise men on one side and the nativity on the other, and I could hardly wait to get to the car and open one end of mine to see what wonders lay inside.

Dad drove us around town to look at the Christmas lights, and when we reached home, he and Jill and I waited in the car while Mom hurried into the house to "check on something," which we all knew was a ruse to give her time to get our gifts ready.

In due course, she told us all to come in, and Jill and I screamed with delight at the pile of gifts awaiting each of us under the tree. They weren't wrapped, because that would be wasteful, although occasionally Mom would splurge and wrap a gift in the comics section of the newspaper.

Our bulging stockings hung over the fireplace, and they were another source of delight. They were huge, and filled with all manner of neat stuff: a new Barbie, an eraser in the shape of an animal, pencils with my name on them, or other trinkets Mom had gotten by sending in proofs of purchase to cereal companies.

***

Two days after Christmas, my sister was born.

Mom loved to report that "Angels We Have Heard on High" was playing on the hospital sound system during her birth.

In honor of the season, she was named Ellen Joy.

Chapter 24 – They'll Know We are Christians by our Love

We are one in the Spirit, we are one in the Lord
We are one in the Spirit, we are one in the Lord
And we pray that all unity may one day be restored
And they'll know we are Christians by our love, by our love
They will know we are Christians by our love

I knew my Ten Commandments from an early age. I also learned the New Testament commandments, the ones about loving God with all your heart and soul and mind, and loving your neighbor as yourself. But somehow, those two didn't carry the weight of the original ten. Maybe it's because it was a lot more clear-cut to remember "Thou shalt not steal" than it was to consider who your neighbor might be.

My sixth grade Sunday School teacher, Mrs. Botkin, was really nice. She let us into her life by sharing tidbits she picked up in her day-to-day reading. Once she told us she'd read that we could increase our brain power by doing small, everyday things in slightly different ways.

I took this to heart, making a real effort to tie my left shoe first instead of my right. Walking home from school, I wove a different path across the kickball field each day. After all, you just never knew what was around the corner, and I figured more brain power could only be a good thing.

I was considering whether to cross my left knee over my right, or vice versa, in class one Sunday when Mrs. Botkin asked Rhoda to pass out pencils.

Rhoda picked up the pencil box from Mrs. Botkin's desk and walked along the row of chairs, handing one to Lisa, to Lori, and to Bekki. She walked right past me without a glance and handed pencils to Laura and a new girl.

I raised my hand. "I didn't get a pencil."

"Rhoda, you forgot Susan," Mrs. Botkin said.

"Oh, I didn't forget her," Rhoda said with a grin and her trademark laugh. "I just don't like her!"

My insides took a nosedive at this humiliation, yet on some level I appreciated her honesty. I had known for years, or at least strongly suspected, that Rhoda didn't like me. Laura didn't either, and while Bekki tolerated me, I knew I would never be her first choice. I wasn't sure why they disliked me, but I had a few ideas.

***

Church choir rehearsal had ended, and I was walking along the curb outside the church, toe to heel, pretending it was a balance beam and I was Nadia Comeneci.

A shadow fell across my path as Laura and Rhoda walked up.

"Well, look who it is … little miss goody two-shoes!" Rhoda greeted me. Mom always told me not to be sarcastic, and I was wishing at that moment that she would show up and remind Rhoda of this little guideline.

Laura took over: "My mom always tells me, 'Why can't you be like Susan?' I am *so sick of it!*"

I looked at them helplessly, my feet frozen to the curb in an odd, vertical line. What could I say to this?

I'm not ***that*** *good. Just ask my parents* … no, sounds kind of snotty.

You shouldn't try to be like me! Just be yourself…nope, too condescending.

I wish we could just be friends and get along … true, but I couldn't muster the courage to say it.

I tried to mentally prepare myself for whatever might be coming next. Would Laura or Rhoda take a swing at me? Would they, heaven forbid, beat me up?

But after ten seconds of awkward silence, which felt like all 40 years of wandering in the wilderness, they walked away. I was left swaying on the curb, sure of why my Sunday school peers disliked me. I was being held up as the dreaded *example.* Being good was doing me no favors.

And despite being the example, I feared I wasn't really such a good one. I thought of Karen, who rode my bus in the morning.

"Greasy hair!" the older boys called out at her, as she stood at her spot on one end of the quiet street. She always looked down and appeared to be intensely preoccupied with the gravel on the ground.

I looked at Karen's hair, and thought that the older boys must have been better observers than I was, because it looked no different to me than anyone else's hair. It was kind of shiny, but wasn't that a good thing? I stood with the others on the opposite side of the street. I knew I should stick up for Karen, but I didn't know exactly how.

I pondered what Jesus would do, but Jesus was, well … *Jesus,* which was a huge advantage. He could've worked a miracle for Karen, or spoken a well-timed word that would've blown her bullies into the next county. I was just me, an awkward preteen who wasn't too many rungs higher on the popularity ladder than Karen was.

In the end, my kindness consisted of slowly edging toward Karen, rather than away from her, as we all stood at the bus stop. It wasn't Cleansing the Temple of money changers, but it was a beginning.

***

Sixth grade meant that Rosebuds had ended. I mourned this fact each Wednesday night as I endured a class that functioned as a poor alternative for P.E. And so I stood either outside the church or inside a classroom, depending on the season, and waited for the teacher to call my number in yet another round of Steal the Bacon.

Most nights, I begged the teacher to let me be scorekeeper, which meant I didn't have to take a turn waiting for her to call my number and dash to the center of the room, competing against another child to be first to grab the "bacon," which was usually the chalkboard eraser. I stood at the chalkboard and made tally marks, missing Aunt Phyllis and Grandma Short and wondering whether I had fully bloomed yet or not.

"Okay, enough Steal the Bacon!" Mrs. Davis called out, mercifully, after awhile. "Let's do some sword drills."

She was greeted by a chorus of "Aww!" The word of God was no match for games that involved running.

"C'mon -- you guys know this is church! Okay, I'd like Donnie and Kelly to be team captains. Go ahead and choose your teams. Ladies first, so Kelly, go ahead."

One by one, Kelly and Donnie called our names and we each walked to our teams. Finally, the only kid left was Phillip. Yes, wild Phillip. But on this particular night, wild Phillip had evidently had enough.

"I'm sick of this!" he shouted at the top of his lungs. "Everybody hates me!" And then, an unheard-of thing happened. Phillip began to cry, right there in the middle of class. We all looked at each other nervously before averting our gazes uncomfortably to the floor.

"Why, Phillip, that's not true!" Mrs. Davis said, looking pretty flustered herself. I felt a lot of sympathy for her, because actually it **was** kind of true. "Everybody here likes you!"

She smiled and tried desperately to establish eye contact with one of us, but no one was biting.

Finally, she had no choice: "Jesus loves you!"

At that, we all looked up again, greatly relieved, because it was undoubtedly true that Jesus loved Phillip. He loved Phillip when he was good, and he loved him when he was bad. He even loved Phillip enough to die for him!

Phillip still didn't look happy, but he got his emotions under control enough to walk over to his team, which greeted him reluctantly.

I had no doubt Phillip knew that Jesus loved him, but right then, I think Phillip wanted an actual human person to love him. Maybe one who was nine years old on a summer Wednesday night at church, just like him.

***

Dad pulled out the Bible Storybook and we pushed our plates aside to hear the night's story.

I hopped up to answer the ringing phone.

"Hello? Um, I think you have the wrong number. Sorry! No, it's okay. Bye!"

Jill grinned. "That's your Wednesday night class voice!" she said triumphantly.

"What?" I asked.

"Your Wednesday night class voice. You always talk different there. Really quiet and nice. Not like how you talk at home at all!"

"I do not!" I countered, trying to salvage my reputation. But now that she mentioned it, maybe I did talk differently at church. I wasn't trying to. And surely no one could be expected to talk in a quiet, sweet, submissive voice in daily life. Well, I imagined the Murk family probably did, but they were a special exception.

"Okay. So tonight's story is about the prodigal son."

Dad went on to read the tale, about the lousy son who was greedy and wanted his share of the money before his dad died, and then wasted it all on profligate living. I wasn't sure what profligate entailed, but from the context I assumed that it meant he was drinking, smoking, dancing, and possibly using drugs, if those were around in Bible times.

Then one day he realized how good he'd had it, and headed back home. His dad greeted him joyously and threw a big party for him. The story ended with the older brother getting all mad because of the party. He told his dad that he'd worked hard, and he'd never gotten a party. Then the dad said that everything he owned belonged to his sons, but that he had to celebrate because the lost son was found.

Dad closed the storybook and offered a rare commentary.

"You know, that's a story I kind of have a hard time with. I can see the older son's point. He worked hard, and yet the dad throws a party for the son who wasted everything and ran away."

I felt the mashed potatoes I'd just eaten sitting like a lump in my stomach, because I felt the same way. I could work up a little sympathy for the prodigal son, especially when he was dining on pig slop, but I didn't like him. He was bad. On the other hand, I felt that the older son had gotten a raw deal. He had followed the rules, and look where it got him: he was cast as the bad guy in a parable told by the Son of God.

I felt bad that I related so strongly to the older son. I wanted to feel more mercy for the prodigal one, but I just didn't.

And like magic, it happened again. I remember the verses about Paul facing the same dilemma: *For the good that I want, I do not do, but I practice the very evil that I do not want. But if I am doing the very thing I do not want, I am no longer the one doing it, but sin which dwells in me.* (Rom. 7:19-20)

I was grateful that even the venerable Paul had faced a similar dilemma. Still, I wished that life could always be as easy as Thou Shalt Not Steal.

Chapter 25 – I Will Sing of the Mercies of the Lord

I will sing of the mercies of the Lord forever,
I will sing, I will sing,
I will sing of the mercies of the Lord forever,
I will sing of the mercies of the Lord.

With my mouth will I make known Thy faithfulness,
Thy faithfulness, Thy faithfulness.
With my mouth will I make known
Thy faithfulness to all generations.

I knew a thing or two about music, owing in no small measure to my frequent attendance at First Baptist, because we sang there. A lot. Each service began with an organ prelude, and just in case there was any confusion, *The Messenger* spelled things out: *Worship begins with the first note of the organ. Service begins with the last note of the organ.*

We'd open the service with a hymn, and there would be several more hymns throughout the service. And I think it was part of the church constitution that we sing all the verses. Usually there were four verses, although there was the occasional hymn with five or even six. Services always ended with a hymn, and of course we always sang a hymn after communion, copying the disciples who *sang a hymn and went their way.*

As one of Seymour's largest churches, First Baptist's Sunday service was carried live on the local radio station. The downside of this was that our service had to fit more or less within the one-hour radio slot. No doubt this hindered the workings of the Spirit at times, especially when it came time for the altar call.

If it was 10:57 and no one had responded during the first few verses of the invitation hymn, Dr. Silver might make a subtle "stop" hand signal to Mom and the organist, letting them know that the chances to stand up for Jesus were done for the morning.

But it wasn't just the clock that put a damper on invitations. Once the Sunday school teacher told our class, "I really think it's wrong that some people in church close their hymnals during the last verse of the altar call. What if the pastor wants to extend the invitation? What if someone would accept Christ as his Savior, if only we'd sing *one more verse*? When you close your hymnal, I think it's just like saying 'I'm done; I'm ready for lunch.'"

Well. This convicted me, because I indeed had been an early-hymnal-closer. After all, I knew all the words by heart. And most Sundays, yes, I had to admit that a fair portion of my thoughts during the invitation hymn did revolve around lunch. Apparently, I'd been stifling the spirit without even meaning to.

***

Sunday night hymn sings were popular at First Baptist. I had it on good authority from Mom that each minister of music loved them, and I can see why, since they resulted in zero planning on his part.

As the service began, he'd announce, "Tonight, we'll be taking hymn requests in a few minutes here. So be thinking about your favorite hymns, and I'll give you a chance to tell them a little later."

Certain hymns were guaranteed to come up: "Amazing Grace," "Just a Closer Walk With Thee," "How Great Thou Art," "It is Well With My Soul," "Great is Thy Faithfulness." And sometimes, there were strange choices (I got a major case of the shivers each time we sang "There is a Fountain Filled With Blood").

Because of the sheer number of hymns being called out, we only sang one verse of each request, but the minister of music had been known to change this rule ("You're all singing so well! Let's continue on to verse two!").

All those years of staring at the hymnal had their reward. Although I had studied piano since second grade, the sheer amount of time spent looking at the music to those hymns improved my sight-reading and musical ability. I learned how to sing the alto line to hymns, if for no other reason than that I was bored with the soprano. Often I'd totally lose sight of the lyrics in fascination with a specific rhythm or chord -- why the B-flat there for the tenors instead of a D? I knew I'd need longer than a dotted half note to ponder this.

Then there were moments when a phrase would so intrigue me that I forgot all about the melody for a verse or two.

Hast thou not seen how thy desires e'er have been granted in what He ordaineth? I hadn't thought of it that way (although I wished that I had), but now that the hymn-writer mentioned it, yes.

Earth hath no sorrow, that heaven cannot heal. Wow. That was deep, and good to know as well.

Once a year or so, the choir would pull out "The Prayer of Saint Francis of Assisi." As I listened to those lyrics, they were so moving that I didn't know if I could stand it.

Lord, make me an instrument of your peace.
Where there is hatred, let me sow love.
Where there is injury, pardon.
Where there is doubt, faith.
Where there is despair, hope.
Where there is darkness, light.
Where there is sadness, joy.
O Divine Master,
grant that I may not so much seek to be consoled, as to console;
to be understood, as to understand;
to be loved, as to love.
For it is in giving that we receive.

It is in pardoning that we are pardoned,
and it is in dying that we are born to Eternal Life.

***

There was nothing special about Seymour's Lutheran Nursing Home. When you walked in the front door, it smelled like Swiss Steak mingled with urine, and there was most likely an old man keeping guard in his wheelchair in the entrance, staring straight ahead.

But each Saturday, Jill and I rode our bikes over to the Home. Mom had arranged for us to volunteer, figuring we could brighten the days of all these folks who were living on borrowed time. The powers that be assigned us to Hettie, a blind lady who apparently appreciated readers. Jill and I arrived for our first day, somewhat nervous, clutching a Bible and a few other books we'd rounded up. Hettie didn't say much when we introduced ourselves, and since she couldn't see us I reached out and stroked her hand. She smiled slightly but looked confused. Who were these strange new people with child-like voices?

"We brought some books to read to you," Jill said. "We've got *Stories from Grandma's Attic*, and *Little House on the Prairie*, and the Bible." Hettie chose the Bible.

And thus began our long relationship. Each Saturday, we walked down the pungent hallway to find Hettie. She was always in the same spot, as predictable as the manna each morning. Jill read for awhile, and then I took over. We always read the Psalms, and it wouldn't be more than a minute or two before Hettie would begin to cry. Not out loud, but tears streamed down her face.

The first time this happened, I stopped with some alarm. My reading had never before produced tears in anyone.

"Oh no," she said, "go on, go on!"

And so we continued, reading *I will lift up mine eyes unto the hills, from whence cometh my help,* and *Wait on the LORD: be of good courage, and he shall strengthen thine heart,* and *O lord, thou hast searched me, and known me.*

Hettie nodded her head a lot, whispered "yes" occasionally, and cried and cried and cried. But she cried the most when we left.

Once a month, Mom joined us. On those days we went to the big room with a piano, and Mom played hymns while Jill and Ellen and I sang, or sat on the piano bench, or visited with the residents. They loved Ellen most, since she was a baby, but their eyes lit up for all of us. I suppose we were considered golden, since we possessed something they visited only in memory: youth.

Mom broke into "Victory in Jesus," and an amazing thing happened. The seemingly comatose man in the corner began tapping his toe. The large lump of a woman parked nearby in a wheelchair, sleeping, opened her eyes and began to sing. And folks everywhere, who'd shown no sign of interest whatsoever, began moving their lips along to the words of every verse.

This transformation continued on into "Love Lifted Me," and "To God Be the Glory," and "When I die, hallelujah by and by, I'll fly away," and I realized that I wasn't the only one with a sixth sense when it came to hymns.

One Saturday, Jill and I arrived to read to Hettie. She wasn't at her normal spot, which panicked us a little because it had never happened before. We walked one long hallway and then another, trailed by Ross, a resident who'd taken a shine to Jill.

"Come on, just one little kiss?" Ross begged, over and over.

"Maybe we should ask someone about her?" Jill asked nervously. But while we were fearless in reading to Hettie, our courage disappeared when faced with the prospect of approaching the receptionist.

We ended up riding our bikes back home. Mom called the Home, and learned that Hettie had died that week.

She'd flown away.

***

Since man shall not live by hymns alone, Jill and I expanded our musical tastes through *The Lawrence Welk Show*. Each Saturday night, we'd head to the living room with Mom (Dad was gone, probably to a ballgame) for an hour with our musical family.

I loved Guy and Ralna, thought Norma Zimmer was lovely but a little too sweet, and secretly wished to be Cissy, the dancing lady. And Bobby, the dancing man, had been a Mouseketeer, which automatically qualified him for star status in my book.

My parents had given Jill and me a joint gift for Christmas, a tape recorder. In my eyes, joint gifts were usually a bad idea, because I felt no ownership in possessing just half of anything. But the tape recorder was an exception, both because it was so expensive, and because it was so neat-o.

Jill and I had a ball recording Ellen's attempts at saying "baby," "Susan" (which was always Toodun), and "Jill" (Dill). We also accosted any visiting toddler-aged children and taped them saying anything at all, so that we could listen to it over and over again later, at least until Mom warned us that we were going to break that thing if we kept it up.

The highlight of our recording sessions was the Saturday night viewing of Lawrence Welk. We didn't want to record the entire show, because parts of it were boring, like when the champagne orchestra played. We only wanted to tape our favorite parts. But this presented a dilemma, because we only got a few seconds when the next act was announced to decide whether it was tape-worthy or not.

"And now, my lovely daughter-in-law Tanya, singing 'Moon River'."

Jill looked at me.

"Boring."

"Yep," I agreed.

I relaxed my fingers on the recorder buttons and sat through the performance.

"Anda now, our dancing pair, Bobby and Cissy, will put on their dancing shoes for 'Singing in the Rain'."

"TAPE IT!" we said in unison, and Jill shouted "Jinx; owe me a Coke!" as I feverishly attempted to push "record" and "play" simultaneously.

I missed watching the first ten seconds of the dance as I waited to be sure the wheels of the recorder were turning, but it was worth it. I could now listen to Bobby and Cissy's dance music anytime I wanted to.

Chapter 26 – This is My Father's World

This is my Father's world, and to my listening ears
all nature sings, and round me rings the music of the spheres.
This is my Father's world: I rest me in the thought
of rocks and trees, of skies and seas; His hand the wonders wrought.

Mostly, God used his still small voice in Indiana. There are other places that have the mighty wind, the fire, and the earthquakes, but somehow the quiet whisper of our cornfields and rolling hills spoke to me just the same. And when God did choose to shout, just a little, like he did with the Jug Rock, he had my full attention.

The Jug Rock was the most familiar landmark along the tortuous road to my grandparents' houses. We knew the two-hour trip was at least approaching an end when Dad called out, "Okay, Jug Rock coming up in about a mile!"

Jill and I always perked up at this and stopped our backseat squabbling over who had touched whom.

"And … there it is!" Dad would triumphantly proclaim, as we'd round the bend and gaze intently out the right-side window at the mighty Jug Rock. It was easier to see during winter when the trees were bare, but sometimes, when the weather was nice, we'd actually stop and explore this wonder just a little.

Jill and I scrambled down the steep ravine, locusts buzzing in our ears and mosquitoes coveting our blood. Our goal was the mighty 42-foot sandstone Jug Rock, and we'd oooh and ahhh over its massive size as well as the miraculous table rock balancing on its top. Sometimes, small trees had sprouted out of this table, and it was almost too much to imagine a God capable of creating such a thing. I didn't much care whether God had made the Jug Rock 3,000 years ago or 300 million. I'd just close my eyes and imagine dinosaurs cavorting around its base, and "How Great Thou Art" didn't seem sufficient to convey all the wonder of the place.

***

The Jug Rock wasn't the only time God used his loud voice in Indiana. He also bestowed tornadoes on us occasionally, or *twisters* as they were called in "The Wizard of Oz." The annual network TV showing of "The Wizard of Oz" was one of the year's highlights for Jill and me, and we settled excitedly into the couch to watch Dorothy's adventures from Kansas to Oz. I knew that "The Wizard of Oz" was made up, but parts of it, like the twister, were true. Living in southern Indiana, I was plenty familiar with twisters.

Every now and then I had surveyed an ominous sky turning gray-green above the cornfield behind our house. The wind picked up, Mom or Dad hollered for me to *get in here!*, and the next hour would be spent anxiously huddling around a transistor radio in the basement. Dad would go up the steps every so often to personally inspect the sky, and when the radio announced that danger was past, our relief was great.

Tornado drills were a part of school life as well. We alternated tornado drills and fire drills, and each had its own alarm bell. Tornado drills required us to take a heavy book and file silently into one of the school's long, window-less hallways, where we knelt along the wall and covered our heads with our books.

These drills were usually ten-minute affairs, but once we had an exception. I was already wary on that day when the alarm sounded, because of the wind and the oddly-colored sky. After twenty minutes spent crouching in the hall without the "all clear" sounding, I knew this was more than a drill.

A constant refrain of "Shhhh!" and roaring wind filled my ears as Mr. Rucker's polyester-clad legs patrolled past, followed by Mrs. Baughman's sensible shoes. We kids were dying to discuss the situation, but of course this was strictly forbidden. Teachers gathered and whispered in groups, then returned to shush us.

The end-of-school bell rang unheeded. The wind continued to howl. My legs started falling asleep, one and then the other, and I longed to get up. But the teachers had told us that the only way this could happen was if we had an *extreme emergency*, in which case a decidedly unamused teacher would escort the suffering student to the restroom.

Finally, thirty minutes after the school day normally ended, we were given the okay to stand blessedly upright, and go home. A tornado had indeed passed over, but mercifully, we had been spared. I viewed this as one of the best days of the school year. A real tornado was a fearful thing, but to live to tell about one I'd actually survived was a badge of honor.

The residents of Seymour weren't always spared. Maybe every third year, a tornado touched down and did real damage. On these occasions, we drove slowly by the damaged houses after church on Sunday, feeling sorry for the owners and yet blessed to have dodged the bullet ourselves. I imagined Noah and his family must have felt much the same when the rain began to pour.

Frequently, a single room remained standing amid the wreckage, quiet and tragic-looking, like Lot's wife after she'd been turned to salt. This surviving room was always in the center of the house, and we heard the repeated admonition: in a tornado, your first choice was to head to the basement. Barring that, you should head to a room in the center of the house.

One September night when I was twelve, the sky had turned the familiar churning green shade. Tornado watches were turning to warnings, but we went on to Sunday night church services anyway.

God made all things, including tornadoes, and he didn't close his house on account of them.

Near the end of the sermon, the deacon of the week interrupted Dr. Silver to whisper a message.Deacons sometimes brought Dr. Silver a glass of water without piquing my curiosity. But whisper to him? This never happened, so I stopped my mental tally of dark brown bricks to see what would transpire next.

"We've just been informed that a tornado is heading this way from Brownstown," Dr. Silver announced. "After we sing our song of invitation, let us seek shelter under the pews."

Jill and I looked at each other, a mixture of fear and excitement on our faces. A loud voice nearby called out, "Well, that'd be about the worst place to be, I mean this big expanse in here. We'd be safer in the corridors, that'd be the best place …"

I was shocked to hear this admonition coming from none other than my dad. Dad didn't "Amen" or even sing much in church, but as a school principal he knew his emergency-preparedness routines, and he was able to take charge in a situation.

Dr. Silver agreed with his assessment, and we hurriedly began singing probably the shortest invitation in the history of First Baptist. Even at that, though, it wasn't short enough for me. In my mind I could see the tornado quickly covering the ten miles separating us from Brownstown, and my teeth began to chatter with a ferocity I'd not known since I was flower girl in my aunt's wedding.

A quick exit from the sanctuary followed the final *amen*, and we made our ways to the numerous and plentiful hallways, passing crying kids and dutifully calm adults. Dr. Silver announced that we were welcome to use the mattresses in the nurseries, and these were a hot commodity. Faces peeked up over the mattresses, which the quickest had grabbed and were using as fortresses against the natural disaster headed our way.

Our family parked itself in a hallway and spent the next hour sitting on the floor in the dark, talking with Miss Fairy and the Batemans. Soon, residents of a nearby trailer park began arriving as well. Tensions ran high, although the novelty of the situation had worn off for several children, whose parents were having a hard time preventing them from treating God's house as a playground.

Finally a congregant announced that he'd heard an all-clear on his CB radio, and we all began heading out into the parking lot, shaking our heads at the still-unsettled sky and winds. It had been a close call, but like the children of Israel when the Angel of Death visited the Egyptians, First Baptist had been spared.

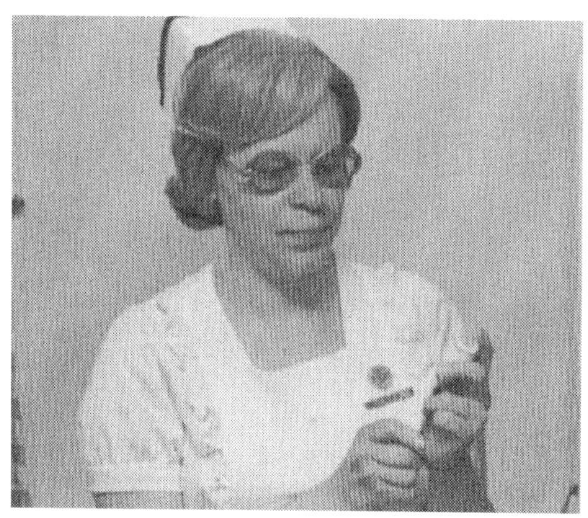

Chapter 27 – Rescue the Perishing

Rescue the perishing, care for the dying
Snatch them in pity from sin and the grave
Weep o'er the erring one, lift up the fallen
Tell them of Jesus, the mighty to save

Rescue the perishing, care for the dying
Jesus is merciful, Jesus will save!

From my earliest days of Sunday school, I knew that Jesus had prepared a wonderful place for me. He had a wonderful plan for my life, if I'd just accept it. Because you know, even if someone buys you a gift, it's not really yours until you take it.

But even after I'd taken that gift and accepted Jesus as my Savior, I still couldn't rest easy. Because there were people -- hundreds and thousands and *millions* of them -- who either hadn't accepted the gift, or who didn't even know it existed! Therein lay my mission.

The Baptist Church was big on missions, and First Baptist was no exception. Missionaries frequently visited on Sunday nights to speak and ask for support. And despite the negative stereotype, I generally enjoyed these talks as well as the slides the missionaries showed -- when they could operate the projector successfully, which was always in doubt. "Jim, could you see if you can run this thing?" was a frequent refrain, and I think knowing how to run a slide projector must have been one of the chief requirements for serving as a deacon. My mom's parents were greatly interested in missions, and the crowning glory of their life came when their daughter, my Aunt Elaine, became a missionary to Africa.

I didn't sense God leading me to Africa to spread the good news, but I was acutely aware of the obligation to share it right in my own little world. After all, I had learned the Great Commission early on: *Go ye therefore, and teach all nations, baptizing them in the name of the Father, and of the Son, and of the Holy Ghost.*

Writing Your Testimony was a frequent topic in Wednesday night class, so that we would all be prepared to *give a reason for the hope that was in us*. The culminating activity was for each of us to share our testimony out loud with the class, but this was a bit of a problem because most of our testimonies had a severe deficit in the conflict and drama departments. The best testimonies came on Sunday nights, when some adult would share how Jesus had saved him from a life of drinking, or smoking, or drugs. The person in question then told how he had accepted Jesus as Savior, usually as a result of witnessing by a church member, and ever after he was an upstanding citizen.

Although I knew that all sin was equal in God's eyes ("It's just as bad to hate your sister as it is to murder," the Sunday school teacher always said, and I'll admit this worried me), somehow my testimony about Jesus delivering me from my coveting of go-go boots and a fur muff just wasn't very compelling for a listener.

There was the further complication that even if I shared my testimony, there was no guarantee that the hearer would take me (or rather, Jesus) up on the offer of salvation. It was more likely that I'd get a strange look, and be branded a *religious fanatic.*

"Do you think it's a little uncomfortable to share with your friends about Jesus?" the Sunday school teacher would ask. "Well, then just imagine how they're going to feel spending eternity in hell. Now that's uncomfortable!"

I had to admit that she had a point.

"Almost persuaded," harvest is past!
"Almost persuaded," doom comes at last!
"Almost" cannot avail; "Almost" is but to fail!
Sad, sad, that bitter wail — "Almost," but lost!

"I think that's just the saddest song," Mom would say, each time we sang "Almost Persuaded," and I agreed with that 100 percent. Between the gnashing of teeth and the bitter wailing and the approaching doom, hell sounded plumb awful, and I sure didn't want to be the cause of anyone ending up there. It was just the actual act of witnessing that was hard for me to work up to.

If witnessing made me a bit antsy, going on visitation was just slightly better. Every so often, an ambitious Sunday school teacher would invite our class to meet at church on Saturday night. She would drive us to visit potential class members, and potential meant that they had visited our class before. Even if the girl in question had only darkened the Sunday school door once, she was forever on the rolls and therefore fair game for visitation.

Mercifully, most of the girls we visited weren't home, or at least no one came to the door when we knocked. When we did get an answer, the conversation was high on the awkward scale.

"Hi, Trina!"

"Hi …" Trina surveyed the vaguely familiar adult and the four girls standing on her front steps.

"Well …" Mrs. Botkin said, "we just wanted to let you know that we've missed you at Sunday school. We sure would love for you to join us tomorrow! We sing and read stories, and we would be so happy for you to be part of our group!"

Silence, and I sent up a little prayer that Trina would be able to come up with an appropriate closing to this uncomfortable little encounter.

"Um … okay." Eloquence was not a common trait among fifth graders.

"Well, okay, maybe we'll see you, then?" Mrs. Botkin wrapped things up, and Trina closed the door. I felt a little bad for her, thinking that maybe the decision on whether or not to go to Sunday school might be a bit beyond her control.

Nevertheless, we had shared our faith and done our duty, and we celebrated by hitting the Dairy Queen. Studying the menu to see what the fifty cents Mom had given me would buy, I decided on a chocolate sundae. However, I forgot that tax was extra, and felt deeply humiliated when the employee wrote down my name, along with "owes two cents" on a little pad of paper.

***

I didn't sense Jesus leading me to Africa, although I wondered about it a lot.

What if he was leading me there, and I just didn't recognize his voice? After all, I knew that *the harvest was plentiful, but the laborers were few.* I asked Jesus things all the time, but I never seemed to get a clear answer. The Sunday school teachers all seemed to suggest the we would "just know" when Jesus wanted us to do something, and I was okay with that when it came to smoking, drinking, or dancing. But what about the questions that were a little more iffy? Did Jesus want me to be a teacher, or a veterinarian? A nurse, or a missionary? I really had no idea, and I didn't know how to discern his will on a whole load of specifics like these.

I knew that he did speak definitively to some people. He had told the revival preacher that 100 people would be saved during the revival, and 100 was a pretty specific number. Was it asking too much for Jesus to send me his will for my life in a concrete way?

The more I thought about it, the more I feared it probably would be his will to send me to Africa after all. Africa seemed to be the place he most always sent missionaries, and it looked like a hot place. Probably even hotter than summer in southern Indiana, and most likely more humid, too. And I doubted that they had hoses in Africa to drink out of. I loved drinking water straight out of the hose on hot days, and to lose this would be a burden, probably just the first of many I'd face as a missionary. The first postcard Aunt Elaine had sent me from Africa, now dog-eared because I'd carried it around so much, showed a woman walking along, balancing a jug of water on her head. I seriously doubted that I had the coordination to do that.

I wondered if maybe God would like me to be a missionary to Europe, more specifically, to Germany. That didn't sound so bad, and I might even fit right in. I suddenly pictured myself hiking in the Alpine meadows, like Maria in *The Sound of Music*, and maybe even becoming a nun. They were sort of like missionaries! But oops, they were Catholic, which was a big no-no.

And the more I thought about being a missionary to the Germans, the worse the idea seemed. I didn't enjoy visitation in Seymour, and it was even worse to imagine myself trotting up a tulip-lined lane to a chalet and knocking on the door. I could imagine a lederhosen-clad man with a handlebar moustache opening the door and leaping back in horror as I opened with a cheery "Guten Tag!" I'd have to invite him to church in German, which would be quite a feat, and suddenly I was very tired of this whole mental scene.

I decided to keep praying for God to show me his will, but in the meantime, I would default to witnessing with my life instead of with my mouth. I vastly preferred this approach, but wasn't totally sure it counted.

Chapter 28 – The King is Coming

The marketplace is empty, no more traffic in the street
All the builder's tools are silent, no more time to harvest wheat
Busy housewives cease their labor, in the courtroom no debate
Work on earth has been suspended as the King comes through the gate

The King is coming, the King is coming
I just heard the trumpet sounding and soon His face I'll see
The King is coming, the King is coming
Praise God, He's coming for me!

There's no question that God was king at First Baptist, but during the 1970s I'd have to say that Bill and Gloria Gaither were prince and princess. Gospel music by the Gaithers was almost always a part of services, and "The King is Coming" was played so often that I knew its lyrics better than my times tables.

"If I have to hear 'The King is Coming' one more time …" Dad grumbled, not to anyone in particular, as he turned the key in the car door after services.

And that wasn't the only one. "Because He Lives" was another favorite, and of course the minister of music, whoever he might be, always instructed "just the ladies!" to sing verse two:

How sweet to hold a newborn baby,
And feel the pride and joy he gives.
But greater still the calm assurance,
This child can face uncertain days because He lives.

Because, of course, you couldn't really imagine a *man* holding a newborn baby.

I can't count the number of times I heard people soloing to "He Touched Me," "The Longer I Serve Him (The Sweeter He Grows)", or "Something Beautiful," and our kids' choir knew every word to "I Am a Promise" (the adults in the audience always smiled indulgently at the kids' cute efforts to sing "I am a great big bundle of … potentiality!").

The Gaithers' music was young and new: hip music for the church-going crowd. It was the perfect repertoire for the First Baptist Church's youth choir.

In seventh grade, the youth of the church became eligible to join New Life Singers. For a time, there was a smaller, more select group as well, The Communicators, which was sort of a show choir with modesty. The girls' gingham maxi-dresses in various pastels captivated me, and although I can't recall the guys' attire, I'll bet it involved pastel leisure suits.

By the time I had reached New Life Singer age, The Communicators had disbanded. This was just as well, as I'd come to the conclusion that I didn't like to sing.

I loved the church hymns -- their words had sustained me throughout my entire brief life. I enjoyed playing piano. But singing I could take or leave. I certainly didn't want to be in the youth choir and sing before the congregation each week, but that's what good Baptist teens did, and Mom was adamant that I do it.

"New Life Singers tonight -- I hope you have your homework done!" Mom announced cheerily. I was sitting on the edge of the patio, shelling peas from the garden. Mom held a lighted match nimbly between her fingers, singeing just the edge of a copy of the Constitution she was "antiquing" to hang over the couch in honor of our nation's Bicentennial. If idle hands were the devil's playground, he didn't stand a chance with Mom.

"Aw, Mom, I don't want to go to New Life Singers!" I whined. I kept myself insanely busy on Sunday afternoons each week, hoping she'd forget.

"For Pete's sake -- ruined this one!" Mom stomped out the match on the patio, shaking her head and staring ruefully at the Constitution. As often happened, the burning had gotten out of control and had wiped out half the signatures at the bottom. "What kind of attitude is that? You need to go and support Reverend Anderson."

I liked Reverend Anderson, the current minister of music. He was smart and well-read, and he recognized my piano pieces ("Ah, the Pathetique!" he said when I played the single opening chord from a Beethoven Sonata. I was forever after amazed by this).

"Can't I support him some other way? Maybe play for one of the kids' choirs?"

"Absolutely not! All the teens are in New Life Singers. You're just as good as any of them, and we're leaving in twenty minutes, so get your show on the road."

I sighed as I dropped another pod full of peas into the bucket. I wondered if all Christian soldiers served a stint in the youth choir.

***

On one or two occasions, my sinfulness led me to flee directly from the car to my favorite church bathroom, where I spent the entire choir session staring at the little children of the world stickers on the wall, and lifting my feet every time the bathroom door opened so that no one would spy me in my stall. But other than that, most every Sunday night of my youth was dutifully spent singing with the New Life Singers.

I slid into the back row next to Rhoda, Laura, and Bekki, who enjoyed the experience about as much as I did. We made quite a surly group, with Reverend Anderson urging us again and again to "Sing out!" as he conducted with more and more vigor, pumping his arms, pushing up his glasses, and wiping the sweat from his brow.

In an attempt to be relevant, Reverend Anderson purchased a book of "new music" for the choir, called "Beyond Imagination." A quick look inside confirmed my suspicions that this was not the type of music that would inspire me.

Jesus, he's beyond my imagination,
And his beauty is beyond my fantasy!
Oh my heart is filled with wonder when I stop to think of him,
For Jesus is my Lord, and King of Kings!

Why were they talking about Jesus and fantasy? I mean, fantasy was dragons or talking animals. Granted, there was that Bible story about Balaam's talking donkey, but that was different. And, "fantasy" needed to rhyme with "kings," and it didn't. Not even close. Where were the soaring lyrics from my beloved hymns? Not in this book, that was for sure. The book's cover was adorned with a multi-colored, psychedelic rainbow. It looked for all the world like something seen on a stereotypical drug trip. Stereotypical, of course, because I had no way to know for sure.

***

May 21, 1978
Dear Diary,
We are watching a 10 film series "How Should We Then Live?" by Francis Shaeffer on Sunday nights. I must admit I could understand it better if Laura was not forever burping in my ear.

There were consolations. Francis Shaeffer's film series detailing Western culture from a Christian perspective was right down Dr. Silver's alley, and it opened my eyes to a whole world of art and beauty that I hadn't even known existed. The films made Christianity seem like it was more than okay; it was the very foundation of history. It was the basis for everything!

But instead of viewing the films in a spot where I could digest all of this, I sat among my fellow New Life Singers. After we blessed the congregation with a musical number each Sunday night, it was tradition for us to file out of the choir loft and sit together in two adjacent pews on the front right side of the sanctuary, a spot forsaken by everyone else in the congregation.

I knew from the start that this arrangement would be a challenge, having often heard my parents tsk-tsking over the youth and all the noise they made on Sunday nights. Now I was one of those youth, and the prospect was daunting. Could I be in the world, yet not of it?

Bekki loved to lean over and give me the plot of the latest Harlequin romance novel she had discovered. Laura, as noted, loved to burp in my ear. And Rhoda just liked to laugh. I tried to walk a fine line, acknowledging each of them just enough to be polite while still taking in all I could from the film.

Inevitably, some of the older ladies who sat behind us would loudly whisper *Shhh!*, and then things would quiet down for a few minutes. Reverend Anderson could also cast an evil eye on us from his seat at the podium, but he was rendered powerless when the lights went out for a film.

Schaeffer spoke of Christianity offering "freedom without chaos." I was ready to sign up, if I could just make it out of the pew.

"And let's close with that great Gaither chorus, 'The Family of God,'" Reverend Anderson announced as the film credits ended.

I'm so glad I'm a part of the Family of God,
I've been washed in the fountain, cleansed by His Blood!

I looked over at Bekki, and Laura, and Rhoda, and shook my head. We were a dysfunctional family for sure, but hey: we were the family of God.

Joint heirs with Jesus as we travel this sod,
For I'm part of the family, the Family of God.

Chapter 29 – Children of the Heavenly Father

Children of the heav'nly Father
Safely in His bosom gather;
Nestling bird nor star in Heaven
Such a refuge e'er was given.

The girls of First Baptist eagerly anticipated seventh grade, because that is the year we became eligible to join Guild Girls, a club designed to create godly young ladies. Since no equivalent existed for the boys, I can only assume that either they were considered godly enough already or no volunteer could be found to teach them.

Mrs. Waltz led Guild Girls, and having two teenage daughters of her own, she related to us pretty well. There were of course exceptions, such as the apocryphal story of a girl asking her whether she liked Air Supply. Mrs. Waltz reportedly answered, "Sure -- I like to breathe!" This never failed to crack us up; adults were just so *not with it!*

At the heart of Guild Girls was the Ideal Lady program. Each of us girls chose a woman in the church whom we considered an ideal lady. Throughout the year, we gave her anonymous gifts and notes, and we revealed our identities to the ladies at a special spring tea.

My first year, there was no doubt in my mind who my ideal lady would be: Mitzi Green. The Greens had just moved to town, and Mr. Green was the new youth minister. Our church had never had a youth minister before, so he was plowing fresh sod.

But the youth program didn't interest me nearly as much as Mr. Green's wife, Mitzi, and his toddler, Jennifer. I spent hours peering at Jennifer through the window of the church nursery. She was cuteness embodied, and so great was my desire to babysit for her that at times I felt my heart would burst.

Perhaps I should have approached her mom, Mitzi, and offered to babysit, but remember? I was ***quite*** *backward.* Just approaching Mitzi Green in the corridor was enough to send me blushing and stumbling into an empty room.

For Mitzi Green was my ideal lady. She dressed well. She was young, even earning the accolade of "Youngest Mother" on Mother's Day at First Baptist, back when that was still considered a good thing. She had an adorable daughter and a husband who didn't seem too objectionable. Each Sunday, I studied the dress she wore and then immortalized it by sketching it in a "Greens' Notebook" that I had created.

One Sunday, Mitzi wore the most striking dress I had ever seen in my twelve years on the planet. It was yellow and white gingham, with a full skirt and buttons up the front. I could only dream of ever looking so … so thin, fashionable, and lovely.

So, Mitzi was an easy candidate for ideal lady. After that year, however, things became a bit more difficult. Although many of the women of First Baptist were fine Christian ladies, probably even embodying most of the Proverbs 31 woman's best qualities, they just didn't spark my imagination in the same way that Mitzi Green had.

Mom suggested several ladies she thought I should admire. One year, my ideal lady was my mom's good friend. Another year, I followed in the footsteps of 90% of all good Guild Girls and chose the pastor's wife. Mrs. Silver was a kind lady of whom I never heard a bad word spoken. My mom once told me that Mrs. Silver had said I had nice legs, "which is unusual in a girl." I would have really preferred a pretty face, but I would take compliments where I could find them. I felt positively toward Mrs. Silver forever after that.

The Guild Girls ended their school year with a trip to House Party, a convention at a small nearby college. The unofficial highlight of House Party was the initiation of new seventh graders on the first night. I wasn't sure exactly what this initiation entailed, but it was whispered about enough that I knew it wasn't going to involve lighting candles and receiving a flower.

No, I had visions of being forced to strip to some level of nakedness, all the while being made to walk through wet spaghetti as I stumbled my way through some sort of horrible dark maze.

During the first night at House Party, I hardly slept. Sometime during the night, I was awoken by a sound. I listened closely: it was pebbles being thrown at the window screen. This continued for several minutes, and then stopped.

"Bekki?" I whispered to my snoring roommate.

"Bekki? Do you hear that?" I was reluctant to awaken Bekki, anticipating that she would be more than happy to jump right into the middle of whatever was lurking out there.

"Forgive them, for they know not what they do," I prayed silently, bracing myself for the older girls to break through our door at any minute.

But when the minutes continued passing with no further action of any kind, I eventually fell asleep. I awoke the next morning, relieved and yet confused.

At breakfast, I heard whispers among the older girls. All I could pick up was that "Susan is so sweet, we just couldn't do it."

I glanced over at Bekki, Rhoda, and Laura, who were sullenly eating their doughnuts, not one bit happy that my *sweetness* had put the kibosh on a night of fun for them.

Chapter 30 – There is a Balm in Gilead

Sometimes I feel discouraged and think my work's in vain,
But then the Holy Spirit revives my soul again.
There is a balm in Gilead to make the wounded whole;
There is a balm in Gilead to heal the sin sick soul.

By eighth grade, our girls' Sunday school group had a reputation, and it wasn't a good one.

Our teacher for the year was Miss Eades, who was almost a clone of Miss Harrington from third grade. Miss Eades was so tiny she looked like a good wind would take her. She was prim and proper, always attired in the floral-print dress that was apparently standard issue for all the women of First Baptist over age 65. Sometimes, Miss Eades pulled out all the stops and wore white gloves and a jaunty matching hat as well. I knew from the first time I stepped into the classroom that our group, combined with Miss Eades, was not going to be a good mix.

My stress level was high and rising one Sunday morning as I tried to pay attention to Miss Eades and be respectful. Next to me, Bekki was decidedly bored. She sought solace in the chewing gum that was her constant companion, and in a rebel move, offered me some. I shoved her hand away and shook my head, wishing like anything that she would leave me out of her mischief.

But Bekki wasn't known for backing down from a confrontation. She unwrapped her gum, popped it into her mouth, and sashayed across the front of the room, throwing the wrapper into the trash can with a showy flick of the wrist. She returned to her seat and crossed her legs, swinging one foot and chomping on the gum.

"So, girls, when Jesus says, 'the hour has come to glorify thy son,' what is he talking about?" Miss Eades looked around the group hopefully, her head shaking slightly.

POP … POP … POP …

"Do you think he might be talking about his crucifixion? Maybe?"

POP … POP … POP …

I twisted in my plastic chair uncomfortably. I knew I should raise my hand and put Miss Eades out of her misery, but I was already a dreaded *example*. If I started monopolizing -- or even participating in -- class discussions, there would be no hope for me whatsoever. Still, I tried my best to plead with the others telepathically: *Please* say something! *Please* answer a question! *Please* do anything to take the attention off of the chewing of the terrible gum!

POP … POP … SMACK …

Miss Eades took a little hop, and finally fixed her gaze on Bekki. I watched them like an episode of National Geographic, because I had a feeling this was going to be a showdown of some kind, a death dance between predator and prey.

With her hands clasped and her head still shaking, Miss Eades asked, "Could you please get rid of your gum?"

"No." Becky looked her straight in the eyes, smiled, and continued to loudly, brazenly, chew and pop. Such sassiness!

"I would really appreciate it," Miss Eades implored. Her head was shaking so much that I thought she must be dizzy. She looked like one of those dogs with the bobbing heads that people put on their car dashboard.

Becky stared at her and uncrossed her legs. She leaned forward, planting her black patent Mary Janes firmly on the speckled tile floor. "I'm not getting rid of my gum, and you can't make me."

At that moment, I fervently wished that the earth would open up and swallow me. I was so embarrassed, feeling that somehow my proximity to Becky connected me with her naughtiness. I felt so sorry for Miss Eades, as well. Sure, she was old-fashioned and out of her element, but did she really deserve this kind of payment for trying to share God's word with a bunch of brats?

The standoff seemed to last forever, but eventually it was Miss Eades who gave in. She looked down, found her place in the lesson book, and did the only thing I figured she could do: carry on.

"Well, girls, so we're talking about Jesus. Do you think he knew at that point that he was going to die?"

It took every ounce of courage I had to part my dry lips and speak up.

"I think he did, then. But I don't think God always lets us know about the bad things that are coming up. That might be too scary."

Miss Eades smiled a tight little smile. "Well, thank you for that. I think you might be right."

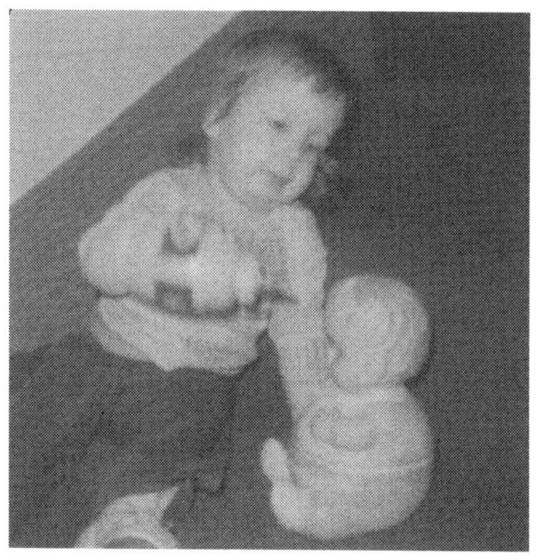

Chapter 31 – Send a Great Revival

Coming now to Thee O Christ my Lord,
Trusting only in Thy precious word
Let my humble pray'r to Thee be heard
And send a great revival in my soul

Send a great revival in my soul!
Send a great revival in my soul!
Let the Holy Spirit come and take control
And send a great revival in my soul!

Once or twice each year, First Baptist Church held a revival. This involved a week when a team of college students, usually from Hardin-Simmons University, came to town, and, well, revived us.

Revivals never failed to stir me, if for no other reason than because of the fresh blood preaching and the fact that we sat in church each night of the week rather than the typical Sunday and Wednesday only. Attendance was emphasized, and often the ante was upped by an outrageous challenge: if 60 teens showed up tomorrow night, the youth revival guy would eat a live goldfish! Sympathizing mightily with the fish, I was greatly relieved when 58 came. I saw this as a win-win, except, I suppose, for the two sinners who missed out.

The revival team usually included a perky young lady who invited all the young folks to come early and participate in games, eat snacks, and, inevitably, watch a sock puppet performance of some type or other. Sock puppets went with revivals like cornflakes went with milk.

Since revival nights included kids' time and often a carry-in church supper as well, they could become lengthy. I learned my 8's in multiplication during one revival week; the pastor's wife quizzed me on them as I walked back and forth along the pew before the service began. I liked 8 times 8 because '64 was the year I was born. And I was unfailingly grateful to be in Mrs. Baughman's class, because we only had to learn up to our 10's. The other class had to learn up to the 12's, which were really hard.

"Susan -- 8 times 7?" Mrs. Silver asked.

"56!"

"6 times 8?"

"47?"

"Close …"

"48?"

"Good job! Okay, I think it's time to sit down now." The organ had begun to play.

Jill brought along a companion to the service that night: her rubber squeeze doll, Plumpy. Plumpy looked like a baby Buddha. Her hands stretched out around her huge stomach and her mouth was fixed in a perpetual grin. She sat on the pew next to Jill and me, and we stole glances at her now and then as we stood, singing the hymns.

"Shall we pray?" asked the pastor, and apparently I was a little too slow to sit down, because my dad grabbed my arm and sat me down -- right on top of Plumpy. Her AHHHH! reverberated throughout the cavernous sanctuary.

Dad was definitely not amused at this, and he shot me a serious evil eye. I was totally humiliated, but apparently others in the congregation were more forgiving. The revival pastor, after closing the prayer, looked up and asked with a grin, "Who sat on the baby?"

He went on to preach about God's plan for our lives, but my mind was occupied with Dad's plan for mine, which I was pretty sure would involve spanking.

***

I was a fainter. The first time it happened, I was in kindergarten. We had just walked back to class after getting our TB tests, and although I was horrified by the sight of the little round tester with all the prickers, I submitted bravely as the nurse stuck it into my arm. I stared at the circle of red dots. They seemed to swirl and stop, swirl and stop, in an odd way. As I stood in line, staring ahead of me at Anita's back, my last conscious thought was, *Well, I think I'm okay.*

My next conscious thought was: *Maybe not.*

I opened my eyes and found myself surrounded by curious classmates, who were all towering above me. The room was spinning weirdly and my ears were ringing. As things began to slow down, Mrs. Wintin helped me up and asked for someone to bring me a milk. I could tell she felt sorry for me, because she opened the carton for me, something we were expected to do on our own as big kids, and she even put the straw in. I sipped, and was conscious of every cold drop running down my throat.

***

My next fainting performance came a few years later, when my teacher had the bright idea to show the class a movie of open-heart surgery. As she slid the big reel onto the projector, she cautioned, "This will be bloody."

Thanks a lot, I thought. I was starting to feel strange even before the film's 5 … 4 … 3 … 2 … 1 … countdown began, and when the surgical instruments began cutting, I knew it was only a matter of time.

The room was filled with a chorus of "Neat!" and "Cool!" from the boys, and shrieks of "Ewww!" from the girls, many of whom put their arms over their faces.

My first line of defense was putting my head down on my desk. But then I thought: maybe I *need* to see this. Maybe it will be on a test.

I took a tiny peek, just in time to see a scalpel cutting into some horrible, pulsating red goo. Black spots began flashing before my eyes, and I knew what was coming.

When I opened my eyes, it was almost like déjà vu: curious and terrified classmates hovering over me, one saying, "She's not dead!" with relief.

The film was stopped for the day, and I spent the next half hour on the cot in the nurse's office, where I felt generally miserable and stared at the big scale.

***

Each revival service ended with an "invitation" during which the congregants were invited to come forward to accept Christ as Savior, or to rededicate their lives to him. This was really no different than any other Sunday service, but somehow the fervor was greater during revivals. One year, the revival preacher shared that the Lord had told him 100 people would be saved that week. This was of course a wonderful thing, but boy, did it put the pressure on the congregation, most of whom were saved already. Revivals always brought lots of rededications, because folks just wanted to do a little something extra for the Lord.

I envied the free-spirited Myers family. They obviously weren't German, because it seemed like at least one of them rededicated themselves every month.

What would it be like to be so responsive to the Spirit? I wondered. And most of all, what was God's opinion on all this? Did he like it when folks rededicated their lives to him over and over, or did he prefer a one-time commitment, even with its inevitable ebbs and flows? I was hoping for the latter, because our family didn't do rededication. We didn't say "Amen" after a hearty sermon either, and we barely even sang loudly. We were Christians, but we were German as well.

Just as I am, without one plea …

I stood in my familiar spot at the end of the pew, next to the aisle, pressing my fingernails into the dinged-up wax on the pew ahead of me. The revival minister of music led us in another round of "Just as I Am," and yet this time it seemed to hold a greater urgency. After the third verse, the revival preacher signaled the piano and organ to pause, and beseeched us: "Brethren, are you listening to the Spirit's calling? Don't stifle the Spirit, my friends. None of us is promised tomorrow." He made a hand motion to continue the music, and on we sang.

I looked around. No one was responding to the Spirit! The preacher scanned the sanctuary hopefully, pleadingly. When no one appeared in the aisle, he called out "Will you come?"

He looked so concerned that I began to get worried that he might cry or totally break down. Why was no one responding? I wished I could respond, but I was already a Christian. I supposed I could go forward to rededicate my life, but I then I remembered I was German and we didn't really do that.

Sweat broke out on the back of my neck, and out of the corner of my eye I could see the ceiling fans spinning, spinning. The music began to sound loud and soft, loud and soft, and then black spots started appearing in front of my eyes. Why wouldn't anyone come?

The next thing I knew, my ears were ringing and I knew immediately what had happened. I really didn't want to open my eyes, so I waited awhile. I could hear many concerned voices around me, whispering. I didn't want them to worry too much, so I finally opened my eyes to a bevy of deacons, their ties hanging down around me like a striped forest.

They were greatly relieved to see me conscious again, and helped me to sit. I, meanwhile, wished I could be anywhere else rather than right there at the center of the entire congregation's attention.

I never learned whether or not anyone responded to the invitation that night, but I did hear whispered guesses on what had happened to me. There was a strong suspicion among some that I had been *slain in the spirit,* although others pooh-poohed the idea, because Baptists weren't slain in the spirit; that was a Pentecostal thing. I had never heard the term, but I knew that slain was the past tense of kill, and I wanted nothing to do with that.

***

Duly concerned, my parents made an appointment for me to meet with a doctor. A specialist, in fact. I was not a bit happy about this. In my mind, things were clear: if I could avoid blood, needles, and emotionally stirring invitations, I was fine. So why had they conspired to bring me to a doctor, in a hospital? I had a hearty dislike of hospitals. The only way I survived that teenage female rite of passage, candy striping, was to serve in the hospital gift shop, far from any actual medical procedures or patients -- although I'll admit that even the large selection of "To Comfort You in Your Illness" cards gave me a slight case of the heebie jeebies.

A nurse ushered me into a room where I met this doctor. Blessedly, he took no blood.

"So. Susan. Are you nervous?" He was staring at his clipboard, and if he looked at me at all, I didn't notice it.

"Ummm … yes?"

Still looking at that clipboard. Whatever was on it must have been fascinating. "How might I be able to tell that?"

What? I thought this guy was a doctor, not a philosopher.

"Well, maybe because I'm swinging this." I gestured toward my little wicker sewing basket, which I'd brought along and was swinging back and forth between my knee sock-clad legs.

"Yes. Very good."

He continued in this manner for a few more minutes, and, with that, my appointment was done.

His report?

"I find nothing wrong with Susan. Perhaps her standards are too high."

My standards are too high.

My standards are too high?

My standards are too high?!

Had this man ever tried to get straight A's? Had he ever aspired to be champion in a 4-H project? For that matter, had he ever read the Bible (you know, *Be ye therefore perfect, even as your Father which is in heaven is perfect*)?

I was so confused with all the mixed messages that I didn't even want to think about it anymore.

***

"So, Mrs. Ford tells me you're Hi C." Mom looked over at me with a conspiratorial smile as she crumbled potato chips over the top of a tuna casserole.

"What?"

"That's what she said: 'Susan is Hi C.'"

I widened my eyes, a look teetering between horror and amazement on my face. "Well, she's wrong! I am definitely **not** Hi C. Maybe I'm Hi C in the 4-H club, but not in real life!"

At my school, we all fell somewhere on the social spectrum. The cheerleaders and football stars were Hi C; the losers and others who disappeared and reappeared at school for reasons no one would discuss were Hoods. While I was far from Hood-dom, I saw myself as equally distant from Hi C. The idea of my 4-H leader thinking that I was a member of that rarified club was a testament to how out-of-it she was.

Because Hi C kids did not sit alone at suppers served after weekly youth choir practice, and I did. This troubled me mightily, and I felt that all eyes must be staring at me as I ate my lunchmeat sandwich in solitude, but I didn't know how to fix it. If this were only a math problem, I'd work until I discovered the answer. If it were a pillow to sew, I'd rip the seam out over and over again until I could get it right. But how to make other church kids like me? This mystified me.

And so I'd take my place at a long table, covered with white butcher paper, and set down my styrofoam plate. And I'd hope someone would join me. But usually, no one did.

Rhoda, Laura, and Bekki congregated together. I'd hear them plan a prank to play on Reverend Anderson after supper. Or maybe they'd discuss which boy in choir was the biggest hunk. I sighed. I had no interest in these topics whatsoever, but I did crave companionship.

The older kids sat together, and *they* were the picture of Hi C. The older kids were cool and self-assured. I hoped to one day be part of such a crowd, but considering my classmates, I couldn't quite visualize how that would happen for our group.

"Mrs. McIntire says the older girls think you're stuck up." Mom burst into my reverie, full of gossip today. Evidently, she had no idea that she was turning my world upside down.

"Stuck up? Why would they think that?"

"Oh, they say you always sit by yourself and you never say much. They just figure that you think you're better than them."

The story of Joshua flashed into my mind; the way the sun stood still on that day, eons ago. That's what this moment was: one where everything as I knew it to be shifted. I was so shy that I would never *dream* of inflicting myself on one of the impossibly-mature older kids. I wasn't sure I could think of a single witty thing to say in their presence. And they thought that I was stuck up? The world was too cruel.

A song went through my head, but this time it wasn't a hymn.

One of these things is not like the others,
One of these things just doesn't belong,
Can you tell which thing is not like the others
By the time I finish my song?

I was a Sunshine Family doll amidst a pile of Barbies. I was the one that just didn't belong, and that felt bad. Very bad.

IRONY, my lit teacher wrote on the board: *a situation in which actions taken have an effect exactly opposite from what was intended.*

"Does that make sense?" she asked. "Can you think of any examples?"

Oh, boy. Could I ever.

Chapter 32 – Jesus, Lover of my Soul

Jesus, lover of my soul, let me to thy bosom fly,
while the nearer waters roll, while the tempest still is high.
Hide me, O my Savior, hide, till the storm of life is past;
safe into the haven guide; O receive my soul at last.

Keith was my first school boyfriend. He was also my last, although I didn't know this at the time. He sat behind me in Miss Wilson's first grade class. I must have outgrown some of my backwardness by then, because I'd frequently turn around, tilt my head to the side, and ask in what I hoped was a cute voice, "How about a little kiss?"

Keith would scowl and put up his fists. But I knew he really liked me.

We had a little bathroom inside our classroom, and Miss Wilson allowed one student at a time to wait at its door when it was occupied. I would stand waiting, doing small dance steps and hoping Keith might take notice of me. I'm not sure he ever did, but once Patrick threw up in that bathroom while I was waiting, and Miss Wilson asked if I would try to clean things up a little while she took him down to the nurse. Cleaning up vomit was much less appealing than waiting flirtatiously, but I did the best I could with a few paper towels.

I was a model student in class, but recess was the magical time to loosen up a bit. One afternoon I tired of playing tag and creating clover chains, and dubbed myself The Kissing Angel. My goal was to kiss as many boys on the playground as I could.

Most of them were less than enthusiastic about this, and I soon found myself face to belly button with the noon duty teacher.

"What's this about you going around kissing people?" she intoned in a way that told me she wasn't charmed by my new identity.

"Yeah … because I'm the kissing angel." Somehow, it lost a lot of its charm when I said it aloud.

"Well, you're not allowed to do that. Go stand by the door."

And thus I was sentenced to the most embarrassing fate I could imagine: standing in shame at the classroom door as each of my classmates filed in from recess, wondering what awful offense I'd committed to land me there.

Throughout my junior high and high school years, I attributed my lack of male admirers to my triple threat: chubbiness, braces, and glasses. But when this deficit continued even after I slimmed down, got contacts, and emerged from braces with no gap between my teeth, I had nothing to blame other than my apparently defective personality.

But it was okay, because Jesus was my boyfriend. Well, not really, but he was the lover of my soul. He loved me more than anyone, and how many earthly boyfriends could you say that about? I talked to him all the time, and yet he never argued back. I had to assume he agreed with me. He didn't buy me flowers or candy, but he had given me his Word. Yes, he had high standards, but I was an expert on those.

Then along came Scotty. Scotty's junior high passion was playing the drums in band, but his high school passion was me. I played piano for the high school choir and Scotty played drums. Usually the choir didn't require any drums, but Scotty came to sit down front anyway, I assume because he just felt more important there than sitting among the singing masses.

After school had been in session a few weeks, Scotty moved from his chair over to the piano bench. He was a big boy, in the horizontal sense, and he smelled of exertion and stale laundry.

"I thought I could turn pages for you," he said in his familiar nasal tone, wiping his dark hair out of his face with one hand and sniffling. Scotty always sniffled.

"Um … okay," I said.

And so Scotty became a fixture on the piano bench with me each day. We didn't talk, but I had to admit that it was handy having a page turner. The only problem was that as class progressed, Scotty kept inching closer and closer to me on the bench. I would in turn scoot farther and farther away, until finally I was just inches from falling off the bench and onto the floor.

"Umm … Scotty, could you please scoot over?" I asked. My arms were so far over from the front of my body that it was difficult to play.

"Sure." And Scotty scooted *closer* to me. I couldn't believe that kid!

"I meant the *other* way!"

"Oh. Sorry." Scotty moved over, and disaster was averted.

Scotty was absent for several days that fall, which was unusual, because he normally had perfect attendance. Then one day, the choir director announced that Scotty's mom had died the night before.

I thought of Scotty, sniffling and glancing at me for the "ready!" signal to turn the page, and I felt so guilty that I wished I could crawl into a hole. I wished he were here at school today, and I vowed that no matter how many times he scooted over, I wouldn't reprimand him.

***

My ambivalent relationship with Scotty continued throughout high school. I can't say that I liked him, and yet I felt sorry for him. I was pretty sure he did like me, and this made me intensely uncomfortable. It also made me ponder why we like the people we do, and what we can -- or can't -- do about it if they don't like us back.

As upstanding members of Future Teachers of America, also known as FTA, we both volunteered to help struggling junior high band students. I'd drive to the junior high each morning for this, and Scotty would usually spot me on my way to the parking lot and come lumbering out, asking if he could ride with me. I'd reluctantly say sure, and I felt guilty yet again for trying to avoid him.

One spring day, I was driving along with Scotty, as usual, basically in silence. Then, he looked over at me and piped up: "Susan, can I ask you something?"

I glanced down at my prized blue fake Nike tennis shoes with the white *swoosh* on the sides. Danger. Danger. Danger, Will Robinson. The way he asked this did not sound auspicious to me. At all.

"Well, okay…"

"Well. You know, the prom is coming up …" Sniffle.

"Oh, gosh. That reminds me. You know that new choir song that the girls' group is doing? 'Big Spender?' I really think it needs drums. Ask Mr. Prout when we get back. I know you usually don't play for that group, but I think that song really needs it. Do you know the one I'm talking about?"

I was grabbing frantically for any conversational diversion I could find, as I sped along the road to the Shield's Junior High, which seemed distressingly far away today. But I did manage to keep Scotty off of the subject for the time being.

***

I did not go to the prom, despite Mom's ominous warnings that "You'll regret it for the rest of your life if you don't go!" This seemed odd to me, since the prom ostensibly involved dancing, which was kind of sinful. Why was my mom pushing it so hard?

She wasn't the only one. One afternoon in May, I was summoned from calculus class to the office. I walked down the steps and then down the long hall, my teeth chattering. What had I done wrong? To be called out in the middle of class was not good.

A kindly older lady counselor met me.

"Come on in, honey," she said, ushering me into her office. This was bizarre.

"You're probably wondering why I called you down," she began, smiling at me.

Um ... yeah.

"We had the names of some really nice students who aren't going to the prom, and we thought you might just need a little nudge to go. So, I have a boy in mind! He's really nice; he's smart. He's in future farmers. He takes hard classes, just like you do!" The woman looked at me with wide eyes, smiling and nodding as she spoke.

At that moment, I wished for nothing more than the Rapture. I felt that dealing with the end times would surely be preferable to this. This woman, who I didn't know from Adam, was insinuating that I was a loser for not going to the prom. And she'd taken it a step further by attempting to match me up with another loser, albeit a decent, smart loser. And I wondered who all was in on this conspiracy. Had all of my teachers discussed my pitifulness as a group? Had my mom called in? It was a low moment, a low moment indeed.

"I appreciate you doing that," I said, my mind frantically trying to think of a graceful exit from this unique little room of hell. "I don't really want to go to the prom. It's okay." I didn't want the nice lady to feel bad, because I could tell that she thought she was doing me the biggest favor in the world.

She stopped smiling, but still looked at me kindly. "Well. If you change your mind in the next day or so, you can just let me know."

She stood up to usher me out.

"You would still have time to find a nice dress. Okay?"

"Um, okay. Thanks."

***

My friend Cheryl planned to be a nurse, but her dream was to do some modeling on the side. However, since the fates are not known for excessive generosity, she kept her expectations reasonable by hoping to be a hand model. "I think my hands look really pretty. Don't you?" she'd frequently ask over lunchtime conversations, and I'd agree casually. Hands were hands in my book, and hers looked good enough to me.

Cheryl and I decided to spend prom night at the movies. The Seymour cinema was showing "Frances," the tale of a '50s actress who ended up in a mental institution. Between scenes of a lobotomy and electroshock, we whispered back and forth, bemoaning the immaturity of boys our age and their inability to recognize our stellar qualities. We were anxious for college, where we were sure all the boys would be wise, witty, and urbane, and Cheryl's hands would lead her to a lifetime of security.

***

I walked across the stage to give the piano a last-minute check before the spring choir concert began. There, on the closed keyboard lid, was a long white box. I knew it must be flowers, and therefore I knew it must belong to Sara, the other pianist, because she had a boyfriend. But a closer inspection revealed "Susan" scribbled on the tag. I opened the box and discovered a single red rose.

I tore into the card.

Thanks for being so nice.
- Scotty

Chapter 33 – Happiness is the Lord

Happiness is to know the Savior,
Living a life within His favor,
Having a change in my behavior,
Happiness is the Lord.
Real joy is mine, no matter if teardrops start;
I've found the secret, it's Jesus in my heart!

I spent my fifteenth birthday party singing hymns. I didn't plan it that way, but it happened anyway, due to my new friend, Missy.

Missy's family had just moved to Seymour, and I knew from the moment Missy walked into band class that I would like her. She was cheerful, and sweet, and nice. People, including me, wanted to be around her.

So I invited her to my birthday party. We all sat around the kitchen table experimenting with makeup samples and then ate a bunch of food I'd made ahead of time, practicing for my 4-H foods project. When it was dark, we sneaked through the field and into the nearby backyard of Mr. K., the good-looking and possibly immoral geometry teacher. Leslie excitedly whispered that she could see his profile through the back window, and then she saw a woman's profile there as well, and things became so exciting that it was all we could do to not just scream out loud. Soon, another neighbor became aware of our presence and came outside, shouting, "Who's that out there?"

Whether this was fact or a rumor, one of us swore that the shouter had a gun, and we took off for my house like Asahel in the Bible, arriving home laughing and exhausted.

I led the group to the living room. How about if party guests told me a song they liked, I suggested, and I would play it on the piano. My mind was racing ahead to the "Theme from Ice Castles" sheet music that I'd spent $2.50 of my own money on. I'd practiced that poignant treble line until it was perfect, and I just knew that my friends would be moved.

"'Can't Smile Without You?'" Leslie asked.

"Sorry, I can't play that one by ear."

"'You Light Up My Life!'" cried Miriam.

"Um, sorry -- I don't have the music to that either."

"How about if we each choose our favorite hymn and sing it?" Missy suggested, with a big smile. This stopped the conversation dead in its tracks.

Miriam didn't go to church, and she shot me a "What on earth?" look, complete with furrowed brows. The other girls were stunned into silence, because really, how did one respond to such a wholesome and heart-felt request?

All I could do was say "Sure!" as I dug the hymnal out of the piano bench and began playing some favorites. Missy sang well and enthusiastically, and even tackled the alto part easily. It was clear that she was experienced at this.

So great was her confidence and all-around niceness that it rubbed off on the others, and soon all of us, Christian and non-, devout and carnal alike, were belting out "Take My Life and Let It Be" with more spunk than the First Baptist congregation usually mustered.

***

That evening planted a seed of covetousness in my mind: why couldn't Missy go to my church? I pondered just how different my church experience might be if she were part of my Sunday school group, along with Rhoda, Laura, Bekki, and the others. The simple addition of one other girl who was excited about serving the Lord might just make a world of difference. I prayed fervently for Missy's family to become convicted that the Baptist Church had an edge on theology over their Nazarene Church, but alas, it never happened.

Those Nazarenes, though, they impressed me.

Sam, another Nazarene and a friend of Missy's, was in Advanced Choir with me. Sam was that rare teen boy: he could sing well, as a soloist, with absolutely no self-consciousness. He was a shoe-in for the lead male role in every musical we did in high school. His slight form made him an unlikely King Arthur in Camelot, but once he opened his mouth to sing, no one doubted that there was *a more congenial spot, for happily-ever-aftering than here in Camelot.*

Sam's confidence went beyond his singing. One day in choir, our director handed Sam "The Impossible Dream" to learn for the spring concert.

I launched into the piano introduction, and Sam's tenor began to soar:

To dream the impossible dream ...
To fight the unbeatable foe ...
To bear with unbearable sorrow ...
To run where the brave dare not go ...

The music and words were so gorgeous, they gave me goosebumps. And here came the big climax:

This is my quest, to follow that star ...
No matter how hopeless, no matter how far ...
To fight for the right, without question or pause ...
To be willing to march into...

"Hold it right there!" Sam stopped his singing abruptly.

Mr. Prout walked up to the stage. "What's the problem?"

Sam pointed to the offending word, namely, *hell.* "I'm not going to sing that."

I was stunned. First, even my high standards would have figured it was okay to sing *hell* in this context, and second, had I really just witnessed someone defy the choir director? Mr. Prout ruled the choir with an iron baton, and I didn't think I'd ever seen him challenged on anything before. I stared straight ahead at a plaque on the piano reading *He who sings scares away his woes* and watched this little drama play out, thankful for the distance separating me from the conflict.

Mr. Prout sighed. And then, amazingly, he said, "Okay. Just sing *to be willing to march on and on for a heavenly cause.* Is that acceptable?"

Sam followed the musical line with his finger. "Yeah, that should work."

And with that, we began the song again.

I was stunned. Just that easily, Sam had confronted Mr. Prout on an issue he considered right vs. wrong. And just that easily, he had won.

Sam and Missy got me to thinking. I realized that maybe it was possible to be happy in the Lord, even in a hostile environment. Because Missy didn't seem to fit in with most of the other girls either, and yet, in her case that seemed more like a positive than a negative. She wasn't consumed with angst over what all of us thought of her. She knew that "Happiness is the Lord" was more than just a song title, and if others didn't want to go along for the ride, well, it wasn't changing her outlook. Sam wasn't afraid to stand up for his beliefs, even when those beliefs were challenged by an authority figure. He had stood his ground, and he had been victorious.

I closed up the "Ice Castles" music, lying open on the piano. I pulled out the old hymnal and played a rousing rendition of "There is Joy in Serving Jesus," all four verses. Somehow, it felt freeing.

Chapter 34 – Give of Your Best to the Master

Give of your best to the Master;
Give of the strength of your youth;
Throw your soul's fresh, glowing ardor
Into the battle for truth.
Jesus has set the example,
Dauntless was He, young and brave;
Give Him your loyal devotion;
Give Him the best that you have.

There comes a day when each little bird must hop from the nest, spread its wings, and fly. For the youth of First Baptist, that day was Youth Sunday. The teens took over on Youth Sunday. They preached, led music, taught Sunday school, and pretty much did everything except clean the bathrooms.

A few weeks prior to the big day, our Sunday school teachers doled out the assignments that they'd chosen for each of us. I started with the simple task of helping in Miss Fairy's preschool class. With a sister 11 years younger at home, this was comfortable to me, and I led the tots to the coloring table and sang "The Wise Man Built His House Upon the Rock" with enough gusto to match any of them.

When a little boy asked me to take him to the bathroom, I grabbed his chubby hand and we were off.

He entered into the stall, while I waited … and waited … and waited.

"Christopher? Are you okay in there?"

Silence.

"Christopher? Are you almost finished?"

"I need you to hold my little thing."

"Ummm … what?"

"I need you to come in here and hold my little thing."

Suddenly his intent dawned on me, and I rushed from the bathroom in horror.

This traumatized me for a decade, but little did I know that things could become even worse.

***

As a high schooler, more was expected of me on Youth Sunday than leading the toddlers. For a few weeks when I was a senior, I faced a gnawing dread that I would be asked to preach. Sure, I was a female, which was ordinarily a disqualification, and yet when I looked at the options in my class from which to choose, I knew that the pickens were slim. When a boy deemed suitably "with it" was announced as Youth Preacher, I breathed a sigh of relief.

But before I'd let it sink in, Mrs. Kidwell read on: "Susan and Rhoda will be teaching the Rebekah Class."

This was a double whammy. I had serious doubts over how well Rhoda and I would fare as a teaching team. In recent years, Rhoda had been in and out of Sunday school. We had been in the same biology class one summer, and when the teacher sent the class outside, Rhoda had seized the opportunity to run away rather than collect leaves for her forestry project notebook. Ever since, she had veered from one scrape to the next.

And the Rebekah Class wasn't populated by cute little kids, but rather by about 20 old ladies. I wasn't worried about any requests they might make of me in the bathroom, but I did worry about most everything else I'd face there.

Nevertheless, I was inspired by the spirit of *whatsoever ye do, do it heartily, as to the Lord,* and I dove into the lesson with enthusiasm -- at least, at first. The lesson was typed in the smallest font I'd ever seen, and it went on for at least ten pages. I didn't want to just read the whole thing to the class, but I didn't think I had the skill to pontificate for an hour, either. The topic was the armor of God. Drawing on memories from Wednesday night class years ago, I considered bringing in a bunch of art supplies and letting the ladies craft little shields of faith, but then that didn't seem like such a good idea.

"Oh, for Pete's sake. They're just a bunch of old ladies. They're not going to eat you, you know," Mom said. "They know you're just a kid. They'll make it easy for you."

Somehow, I wasn't so sure. I rolled a piece of paper into the typewriter and typed up ten questions from the lesson, correcting each mistake with correction paper before cutting them each apart to give to my students. I figured that if I handed out the questions at the beginning of class, the ladies would surely be confident in giving answers.

***

Rhoda and I entered the Rebekah classroom and faced our charges: five rows of older women, sitting in folding chairs. I had never seen such a sea of floral print dresses and sensible shoes, or smelled such a strong mix of Avon colognes, in my life. The women were sitting in total silence, and seemed to regard Rhoda and me with the same interest they would give to a couple of squirrels running by the window.

"Hey there, I'm Rhoda!" Rhoda jumped right in with a big grin, a giggle, and a goofy little wave.

"And I'm Susan, and we're going to be teaching your class today!" I added. I'd worn the new wrap skirt I had sewn, hoping to make a cheery impression on the group, but things weren't looking too promising. The Rebekahs stared at us as if we were just extensions of the little Christian flag mounted on the desk. *I can do all things through Christ who strengthens me,* I thought. It was my Christian version of the little engine that could's mantra.

"So, our lesson is about the armor of God. Do you know anything interesting about the armor of God that you'd like to share?"

Silence.

Alrighty, then. On to another tactic.

"Well, in the teacher's book it gives some background information about the different pieces of armor that I thought was kind of interesting ..." and I was off, reading the book. It hadn't been my first choice, but I felt driven to it.

Rhoda handed out the questions. I sure hoped she was choosing the ladies who looked friendliest and most talkative, although in this crowd that was hard to judge.

I paused to catch my breath, and Rhoda decided she wanted to do a little teaching as well.

"The armor of God. Yeah, it's kind of like makeup."

If this was meant to stir up a little interest among the ladies, it appeared to have failed.

"Because, you know what they say, 'If a barn needs paint, paint it.' That's why I like to wear makeup. And, it's like the armor of God. If you need it, then you should use it, you know?"

I wasn't sure I did know, but neither did the ladies. I forged ahead.

"Okay, so the first question is, 'What are some things a soldier would need to protect his head from?' What do you think?"

Nothing. I looked up, scanning the crowd for whoever had question one to show some type of acknowledgement, but it didn't happen.

"Ummmm. Does anyone have question number one?"

A woman in the back row finally responded, "Honey, I've got it, but I don't really know."

"Okay then, well, does anyone know? Why a soldier might need to protect his head?"

I could hear the second hand on the big wall clock. Tick ... tick ... tick ... tick.

Suddenly, I began sympathizing with Moses. It couldn't have been easy leading those Children of Israel. But although they did a lot of awful things, like complaining about the food and worshiping a golden calf, at least they said something! I wished fervently for the Rebekahs to complain, or talk amongst themselves, or even chew gum. Anything to stop the awful, unending silence.

Eventually, all 60 minutes of the class passed, and the women filed out as silently as they'd sat there.

I looked at Rhoda. "Man, I thought that went well!" she said. This time I was the one who laughed, because it was the only thing I could do. Perhaps my standards were just too high.

***

For the Sunday night service, I was chosen to be church pianist. I was always church pianist on Youth Sunday, mostly by default because I was the only teen who'd stuck with piano lessons past the grade three books. Playing along to my favorite hymns was a cinch, certainly a piece of cake compared to leading the Rebekahs.

The congregation was a much easier crowd than the Rebekahs had been. They gave the Youth Preacher frequent and hearty Amen!'s as he read through his sermon in a heartfelt way.

I was ready to exercise some advanced pianistic skills during the invitation. For I'd learned from years of observation that the invitation was when the musicians had to really pay attention. During the service, we sang hymns straight through with all the verses. But the altar call was tied to the movings of the Spirit, which were hard to predict. Sometimes, usually if the service ran long, the Spirit might truncate the invitation hymn after just a verse or two. But if the Spirit was really moving and a person or two had responded by coming forward, the pastor might extend the invitation, even singing the first verse a second time.

While the Pastor had a direct line to the Spirit, the pianist had to get the news second-hand. Lately I had been studying the pastor closely, watching his hand signals. I recognized the rolling "keep 'er going" to continue, or an open-handed "stop" to wrap it up.

But on Youth Sunday evening, the Youth Preacher did a straightforward once-through of "Just As I Am," with no hand signals at all. I was a little disappointed, but I supposed the Spirit was letting the preacher off easy. Clearly, the Holy Spirit was not a Rebekah.

Chapter 35 – Blest Be the Tie That Binds

Blest Be the Tie That Binds
Our Hearts in Christian Love;
The fellowship of kindred minds
Is like to that above.

Senior year was a little like the Second Coming. It had been so long anticipated that when it finally did arrive, there was a sense of disbelief.

By virtue of their final-year status, the seniors at First Baptist were granted a special privilege for the year: a co-ed Sunday school class.

"I can't wait to have Sunday school with the boys!" Lori said, almost inaudibly. It was one of the few things I'd ever heard her, or her equally quiet sister Lisa, say.

But we girls greatly overshadowed the boys in class, probably because they were justifiably afraid of us.

Mrs. McIntire was our teacher, and I liked her. She had five kids of her own, so she'd been around the block with teens for years, and she had no drama whatsoever. She didn't dress especially nicely or especially badly, and she didn't try to be a cheerleader for God. She just laid the facts out there and let us make of them what we would.

The younger teens all coveted the senior Sunday school room. It was the largest classroom off the Fellowship Center, and it was furnished not with the standard issue folding aluminum chairs, but with couches and formerly comfy chairs cast off by members of the congregation. The brick walls were painted by the youth and shone with peace signs and simple Biblical scenes.

Here we did much the same things we'd been doing for the first 17 years of our lives -- looked up Bible passages, answered questions in our workbooks, and pondered the will of God. This last was a nagging issue in my mind. I thought about it last thing before falling asleep and first thing when I work up.

Which college did God want me to attend? What should I major in? These questions were made even stickier because I didn't even know the answers I'd choose myself, let alone what God was thinking. I prayed fervently, asking God to please, please make an exception to his usual vague method of guidance and just drop me a note out of heaven. Was it so much to ask for one little burning bush moment from the one who made the whole universe?

Once a guest pastor preached to us on Psalm 100:4: *Enter his gates with thanksgiving, and his courts with praise*. He told us that the key to getting into God's gates was to thank him. Then, our next step was to enter the courts because those were closer. The way to do that was to praise him.

I liked that: a formula! I made a list of five things to thank God for, and five to praise him for, although I found the idea of praise a little nebulous. How exactly could I praise God? Did that involve thanking him for all his omni's (omniscient, omnipresent, omnipotent, omni-whatever else)? If I praised a friend, it would probably involve telling her that she was great at math or piano, but somehow telling God that he was great at creating seemed a little contrived and condescending on my part.

Still, I loved the how-to aspect, and I wished for that preacher to return and do a follow-up on a verse that would tell me how to discover God's will for my life.

"I don't know how to figure out what God's will for me is!" I asked from my spot on the sagging couch. I hesitated to bring up such a personal issue in Sunday school, but I figured that I was a senior and time was running out. I only had three weeks to decide whether to attend Purdue or Indiana University, and nothing from God had arrived in the mail.

"I don't think it's that big of a deal, really," Mrs. McIntire replied calmly.

I looked at her as if she'd just used God's name in vain. Determining God's will wasn't a big deal? It was the only deal! I was spending a huge part of my prayers in the effort to discern it.

"You just take the next step," she continued. "If you live your day-to-day life in a way that pleases him, you won't miss God's will."

This was a revelation to me. Could it really be that easy? I sank into the loose springs and considered this while the rest of the class moved on. I wondered if maybe my standards *were* too high. Maybe not too high for God, but too high in expecting how he might speak. Maybe I was expecting a burning bush, when most of everyday life was more of a still, small voice. I pushed a long, slow, breath through my lips. This was big.

***

Senior Sunday 1983 finally arrived. The invitation was over, and Dr. Silver headed back to the podium.

"Friends, on this special day we'd like to honor our graduating youth, who we've had the privilege of watching grow up these last years. I'd like to invite them up to here so that we can recognize them each with a small gift."

We rose from the pew where we had been seated, one last time, in a show of solidarity. Rhoda wobbled up in some insanely high ankle-strap shoes, giggling. Bekki followed her, for once having no gum. Lisa and Lori kept their heads low as they made their way up the steps, and Laura, pregnant, walked up gingerly after them. I finished out the group, stepping up in the pink copy of Princess Diana's wedding dress I'd made specially for senior year events. The ruffle around the bottom was 25 feet long, the same length as Diana's train had been. I doubt that Diana had ever donned a frock with more pride, even while I feared that I looked a little like Glinda the Good Witch in all this finery. The boys meekly followed us up.

I looked down the row at our group. The moments we'd shared over the last 18 years flooded my mind in a tidal wave, like that movie people report seeing in near-death experiences, where their whole life passes before them. I remembered the events, and I felt the emotions, too. And when everything settled, all that was left was an unexpected affection for the wildly disparate, imperfect, unforgettable girls who had traveled this road with me. Our friendship over the years had been an arranged marriage rather than a love match, but we had made it work, one Sunday at a time.

Dr. Silver smiled his benevolent smile at each of us as he walked down the line, shaking our hands and presenting us with our very own copies of Halley's Bible Handbook, personally inscribed by him. My heart did a little flip as I realized that this was really it. My parents had saved up to send me to Ee-ah-rope this summer to play oboe in the Sound of America Band. Then it was off to college, seeking God's will one day at a time. How had my days at First Baptist come to an end? There'd been so many of them, yet they now seemed too few.

"Let's close our service with 'Blest Be the Tie,' in honor of these fine young people," Dr. Silver said with a smile. If he was feeling sentimental, he was hiding it well. Maybe, given the reputation of our class, he was just relieved.

Blest Be the Tie That Binds
Our Hearts in Christian Love;
The fellowship of kindred minds
Is like to that above.

I peered into the congregation. Dad was there, not really singing, but moving his lips like a good German. Jill was gazing with awe at us "big kids" on stage, and Ellen was clutching Plumpy.

And over at the piano, Mom was playing her heart out, adding in some extra riffs between the verses.

Before our Father's throne
we pour our ardent prayers;
our fears, our hopes, our aims are one,
our comforts and our cares.

So many familiar faces looked up at me. Miss Fairy, probably tired from singing "Only a Boy Named David" with a new set of toddlers. Aunt Phyllis and Grandma Short, smiling like a million dollars and wearing flashy silk corsages. Miss Eades and Miss Harrington, looking so put-together in their floral print dresses and pillbox hats. Mrs. McIntire, smiling slightly and looking like God's will was as easy to find as her car keys.

We share each other's woes,
our mutual burdens bear;
and often for each other flows
the sympathizing tear.

Mrs. Gilbert beamed, her bright lipstick as vivid as ever, and I was sure she'd give me permission even now to leave the podium to go to the bathroom, if I asked. The Greens were smiling too, and Jennifer waved up at me in the cutest way.

When we asunder part,
it gives us inward pain;
but we shall still be joined in heart,
and hope to meet again.

And then, a most amazing thing happened. You might even call it a miracle. From a pew, way over on the right hand side, I spotted a bunch of the Rebekahs, sitting in a group. And they weren't frowning. In fact, a few had mild smiles on their almost-parted lips.

These were my people. And I saw them, and behold, they were very good. They'd watched me grow up, and each had nurtured my faith, in a unique way. They'd seen me through loneliness to camaraderie, through doubt to assurance, and through fear to contentment. And now that it was time to go, I felt a little reluctant, like Dorothy when it was time to return to Kansas. *There's no place like home,* I thought. *And this is home.*

Chapter 36 – Amazing Grace

Amazing Grace, how sweet the sound,
That saved a wretch like me.
I once was lost but now am found,
Was blind, but now I see.

The summer after we graduated, Laura had a baby boy. I drove to the downtown children's boutique that was going out of business and bought him the cutest little pair of overalls I'd ever seen.

It was with more than a touch of anxiety that I walked up the steps to Laura's house and rang the doorbell.

Laura came to the door, but she didn't look resentful or threatening. Mostly, she just looked tired.

"Hi," she said, inviting me in.

"I just wanted to bring you a baby gift." I smiled as Laura handed her newborn over to me.

She pulled off the ribbons and paper, and grinned at the overalls. "They are so cute! I can't wait to put them on him. Thanks!"

"You're welcome." I patted the baby on the back a few times. It was a good thing I'd had all those years of babysitting training, because what she said next could have caused a less experienced person to drop him right on the floor. Laura stared at me, and her eyes looked kind of funny, maybe like they were shining slightly. She opened her mouth, and said something that I never would have guessed, not in a million years.

"I have always admired you so much. I wish I could have been like you."

I was so stunned that I couldn't think of a thing to say. Laura admired me? She wanted to be like me? If this could be so, maybe other things could be as well.

Maybe everyone who liked Jesus would be okay.

Maybe folks would know we were Christians by our love.

Maybe I could be happy in Jesus, and maybe I could stand up for him, even if nobody else did.

Maybe I could discover God's will for my life. I had a feeling I was already on the right path.

And all around me, I sensed something.

It felt like amazing grace.

THE END

MOM'S SPECIAL CHEESECAKE

Cheese Cake a recipe I got from a coworker at Holland Custard & Ice Cream, Holland, Indiana around 1959 – 1961.

8 oz. cream cheese, softened
1 normal size box lemon Jello
1 c. hot water
1 normal size evaporated milk
1 c. sugar
1 t. vanilla
graham crackers

Fix Jello with 1 c. of hot water. Let it just begin to thicken. Do NOT let it totally thicken or the recipe will be a fizzle.

Whip the evaporated milk with a mixer. Then add the partially thickened Jello & softened cream cheese, (broken up with a fork), sugar & vanilla. Whip together 'til smooth.

Pour into pan covered with finely rolled graham crackers. Sprinkle more crushed graham crackers on top. Let chill overnight. It is better than if you eat it immediately.

(make it pretty much like I said – sometimes it turns out better than others and I think the Jello thickness is a key factor.)

97837721R00116

Made in the USA
Middletown, DE
07 November 2018